I0409747

S. Hrg. 114–214

MARITIME SECURITY STRATEGY IN THE ASIA-PACIFIC REGION

HEARING

BEFORE THE

COMMITTEE ON ARMED SERVICES UNITED STATES SENATE

ONE HUNDRED FOURTEENTH CONGRESS

FIRST SESSION

SEPTEMBER 17, 2015

Printed for the use of the Committee on Armed Services

Available via the World Wide Web: http://www.fdsys.gov/

U.S. GOVERNMENT PUBLISHING OFFICE

99–603 PDF WASHINGTON : 2016

For sale by the Superintendent of Documents, U.S. Government Publishing Office
Internet: bookstore.gpo.gov Phone: toll free (866) 512–1800; DC area (202) 512–1800
Fax: (202) 512–2104 Mail: Stop IDCC, Washington, DC 20402–0001

COMMITTEE ON ARMED SERVICES

JOHN McCAIN, Arizona, *Chairman*

JAMES M. INHOFE, Oklahoma
JEFF SESSIONS, Alabama
ROGER F. WICKER, Mississippi
KELLY AYOTTE, New Hampshire
DEB FISCHER, Nebraska
TOM COTTON, Arkansas
MIKE ROUNDS, South Dakota
JONI ERNST, Iowa
THOM TILLIS, North Carolina
DAN SULLIVAN, Alaska
MIKE LEE, Utah
LINDSEY GRAHAM, South Carolina
TED CRUZ, Texas

JACK REED, Rhode Island
BILL NELSON, Florida
CLAIRE McCASKILL, Missouri
JOE MANCHIN III, West Virginia
JEANNE SHAHEEN, New Hampshire
KIRSTEN E. GILLIBRAND, New York
RICHARD BLUMENTHAL, Connecticut
JOE DONNELLY, Indiana
MAZIE K. HIRONO, Hawaii
TIM KAINE, Virginia
ANGUS S. KING, JR., Maine
MARTIN HEINRICH, New Mexico

CHRISTIAN D. BROSE, *Staff Director*
ELIZABETH L. KING, *Minority Staff Director*

(II)

CONTENTS

MARCH 25, 2015

(III)

MARITIME SECURITY STRATEGY IN THE ASIA–PACIFIC REGION

THURSDAY, SEPTEMBER 17, 2015

U.S. SENATE
COMMITTEE ON ARMED SERVICES
Washington, D.C.

The committee met, pursuant to notice, at 10:02 a.m. in Room SH–216, Hart Senate Office Building, Hon. John McCain, chairman of the committee, presiding.

Committee Members Present: Senators McCain [presiding], Inhofe, Ayotte, Fischer, Cotton, Ernst, Tillis, Sullivan, Lee, Reed, Nelson, Manchin, Shaheen, Gillibrand, Donnelly, Hirono, Kaine, and King.

OPENING STATEMENT OF SENATOR JOHN McCAIN, CHAIRMAN

Senator McCAIN. Well, good morning.

The Senate Armed Services meets today to receive testimony on the U.S. policy in the Asia-Pacific region.

I want to thank our distinguished witnesses for appearing before us today and for your continued service to the Nation.

America's national interests in the Asia-Pacific region are deep and enduring. We seek to maintain a balance of power that fosters a peaceful expansion of free societies, free trade, free markets, and free commons, air, sea, space, and cyber. These are values that we share with increasing numbers of Asia's citizens. For 7 decades, administrations of both parties have worked with our friends and allies in the region to uphold this rules-based order and to enlist new partners in this shared effort, an effort that now extends to states like Indonesia and Vietnam.

No country has benefited more from a peaceful regional order in the Asia-Pacific region than China. I am betraying my advanced age when I say that I still remember being in the Great Hall of the People on the occasion of the normalization between our countries. Since then, China's social and economic development has been remarkable, and it has added to the prosperity of the world.

Unfortunately, we increasingly see a pattern of behavior from China that suggests that some of our highest hopes for our relationship are not materializing and that call into question for nations across the Pacific whether China's rise will, in fact, be peaceful. Indeed, many of these troubling activities have only increased under the leadership of the new president, who will arrive here next week for a state visit.

China's military modernization continues with its emphasis on advanced systems that appear designed to project power, counter

(1)

U.S. military capabilities, and deny the United States the ability to access and operate in the western Pacific. At the same time, cyber attacks against the United States are growing in scope, scale, and frequency. Billions of dollars' worth of intellectual property, including sensitive defense information, have been stolen. Many of these attacks, especially the recent breach at the Office of Personnel Management, are believed by everyone to have originated in China despite the administration's unwillingness to say so.

These growing threats are compounded by China's assertion of vast territorial claims in the East and South China Seas, which are inconsistent with international law. In 2013, Beijing proclaimed an air defense identification zone over large portions of the East China Sea, including over territory claimed by Japan and South Korea. More recently China has reclaimed nearly 3,000 acres of land in the South China Sea, more than all other claimants combined and at an unprecedented pace. Last month, China's foreign minister said it had halted these activities, but recently released satellite images show clearly that this is not true.

What's more, China is rapidly militarizing this reclaimed land, building garrisons, harbors, intelligence and surveillance infrastructure, and at least three airstrips that could support military aircraft. With the addition of surface-to-air missiles and radars, these new land features could enable China to declare and enforce an air defense identification zone in the South China Sea and to hold that vital region at risk.

China is incrementally and unilaterally changing the status quo through coercion, intimidation, even force. Its goal appears clear: the assertion of sovereignty over the South China Sea, a key economic artery through which approximately $5 trillion in ship-borne trade passes every year. As one Chinese admiral recently told a conference in London about the South China Sea, quote, it belongs to China.

The United States has rightly rejected this view. As Secretary of Defense Ash Carter said in May, ''turning an underwater rock into an airfield simply does not afford the rights of sovereignty or permit restrictions on international air or maritime transit.'' Secretary Carter vowed that ''the United States will fly, sail, and operate wherever international law allows, as U.S. forces do all over the world.''

Unfortunately, it has been 4 months since that speech, but the administration has continued to restrict our Navy ships from operating within 12 nautical miles of country's reclaimed islands. This is a dangerous mistake that grants de facto recognition of China's manmade sovereignty claims. These restrictions have continued even after China sent its own naval vessels within 12 nautical miles of the Aleutian Islands as President Obama concluded his recent visit to Alaska.

After that incident, United States officials emphasized that the Chinese ships did not violate international law, which allows countries to transit other nations' territorial seas under what is called innocent passage. That is true, but we have not been asserting our rights just as forcefully. We must uphold the principle of freedom of the seas for commercial and military purposes on, under, and below the water. The best sign of that commitment would be to conduct freedom of navigation operations within 12 nautical miles of China's reclaimed islands in the South China Sea.

More broadly, the United States must continue to sustain a favorable military balance in the Asia-Pacific region. We must remain clear-eyed about the implications of China's rapid military modernization. We must take advantage of new and emerging technologies to preserve our ability to project power over long distances and operate in contested environments. We must invest in enhancing the resilience of our forward-deployed forces. We must continue to help our allies and partners in the Asia-Pacific region to build their maritime capacity, an initiative that this committee seeks to further in the fiscal year 2016 National Defense Authorization Act [NDAA]. None of this will be possible, however, if we continue to live with the mindless sequestration and a broken acquisition system.

All of us want to ensure that we avoid miscalculation, but we only encourage miscalculation when there is a gap between our words and our actions. It is that gap that China has exploited to assert vast territorial claims, bully its neighbors, destabilize the region, and challenge the freedom of the seas.

Ultimately, we need to think anew about deterrence. When it comes to China's destabilizing activities, it is not that the United States is doing nothing. It is that nothing we are doing has been sufficient to deter China from continuing activities that the United States and our allies and partners say are unacceptable, the cyber attacks, the economic espionage and theft, the land reclamation, the coercion of its neighbors, and the assertion and attempted enforcement of vast, unlawful territorial claims. We need to develop options and act on them to deter these admittedly unconventional threats or else they will continue and grow. They will do so at the expense of the national security interests of the United States, the peace and stability of the Asia-Pacific region, and a rules-based international order.

With that, I look forward to the testimony of our witnesses today. Senator Reed?

STATEMENT OF SENATOR JACK REED

Senator REED. Well, thank you very much, Mr. Chairman. Let me first thank you for calling this important hearing on maritime security in the Asia-Pacific region and also thank the witnesses for appearing today. Thank you, gentlemen, for your service to the Nation, to the Navy. Thank you both.

When Senator McCain and I were in Vietnam, we heard concern from almost every single government official about the heightened tension in the South China Sea caused by China's activities. Vietnam is not alone in this regard. For the last 2 years, China has undertaken extraordinary and unprecedented reclamation activities on disputed land features in the South China Sea that have alarmed all of the countries in the region, most of which would prefer to resolve these territorial disputes through legal means under the United Nations Convention on the Law of the Sea. These activities appear to have just been the beginning as China has now turned to militarizing these features by building airstrips and surveillance towers that I believe will further destabilize the region.

4

While there has been some progress on the bilateral strategy to decrease tension between the United States Navy and the Chinese Navy for the establishment of new risk reduction mechanisms, such as engagement rules to air and maritime safety, our efforts to date do not seem to have had an impact on China's aggressive tactics in the South China Sea. I would like to hear from the witnesses on what the Department believes is the best way forward to address this activity and whether current efforts are sufficient to deescalate tension and convince the Chinese Government to pursue a legal and diplomatic solution to its territorial disputes with its neighbors.

I am also quite concerned with North Korea's recent rhetoric that it is improving its nuclear arsenal in, quote, quality and quantity, further contributing to the heightened tensions in the region. Admiral Harris, I would especially like to get your assessment and update on the threat posed by the North Koreans and how we are addressing it.

With that, gentlemen, I look forward to your testimony.

Senator MCCAIN. I welcome the witnesses. Secretary Shear, it is nice to see you again and thank you for your continued outstanding service, including as our Ambassador to Vietnam. Admiral Harris, I know that you are relatively new in your job, and we thank you for the great job you are doing. We look forward to your testimony. We will begin with you, Mr. Secretary.

STATEMENT OF THE HONORABLE DAVID B. SHEAR, ASSISTANT SECRETARY OF DEFENSE FOR ASIAN AND PACIFIC SECURITY AFFAIRS, U.S. DEPARTMENT OF DEFENSE

Secretary SHEAR. Thank you very much, Mr. Chairman, thank you, Ranking Member Reed, and all the members of the committee for inviting me to join you today.

I am particularly pleased to be here discussing the Defense Department's maritime security strategy for the Asia-Pacific region and to be alongside our very capable U.S. Pacific Commander, Admiral Harry Harris.

Last month, the Department of Defense released a report detailing its Asia-Pacific maritime security strategy, which reflects both the enduring interest the United States has in the Asia-Pacific and the premium we place on maritime peace and security in this critical part of the world. This strategy is one element of the United States Government's larger comprehensive strategy to uphold maritime security in the Asia-Pacific region and protect America's principle interests in international law, freedom of navigation, unimpeded lawful commerce, and peaceful resolution of disputes.

For 70 years, United States military presence in the Asia-Pacific has played an indispensable role in undergirding regional peace, stability, and security and will continue to protect these interests in the future.

There are, as you know, growing challenges in maritime Asia, trends and behaviors that we detailed in the strategy report. Regional military modernization has increased significantly the potential for dangerous miscalculations or conflict in the maritime domain. Strong nationalist sentiments inflame passions over territorial disputes and discourage good faith negotiations to resolve them. Competition abounds over significant but finite natural resources. In the South China Sea, China has almost completed large-scale efforts to reclaim land and construct artificial islands on disputed features in the Spratly Islands.

While land reclamation is not new and China is not the only claimant to have conducted reclamation, as the chart to my right shows, China's recent activities far outweigh other efforts in size, pace, and effort. We are concerned about China's long-term intentions for these features and the potential for further militarization of the South China Sea. As we have stated clearly to the Chinese, these actions are not only unilaterally altering the status quo, they are also complicating the lowering of tensions and the peaceful resolution of disputes.

Let me be clear. The Defense Department is not standing still in the face of these challenges. We are systematically implementing a long-term strategy aimed at preserving United States interests and military access, building the capability of our allies and partners, and preserving the stability of the Asia-Pacific domain. The Department's strategy comprises four lines of effort.

First, we are strengthening our military capacity to ensure the United States can successfully deter conflict and coercion and respond decisively when needed. DOD [Department of Defense] is investing in new cutting-edge capabilities, deploying our finest maritime capabilities forward, and distributing these capabilities more widely across the region.

Second, we are working together with our allies and partners from Northeast Asia to the Indian Ocean to build their maritime capacity. We are building greater interoperability and developing more integrated operations with our allies and partners. We are also expanding our regional exercise program with a particular focus on developing new multilateral exercises and expanding training with Southeast Asian partners.

The Defense Department is also implementing a new Southeast Asia maritime security initiative. This effort will increase training and exercises, personnel support, and maritime domain awareness capabilities for our partners in Southeast Asia.

On that note, I would like to express our thanks and appreciation to the members of this committee for their work to include a South China Sea-focused maritime capacity- building authority in their draft of the fiscal year 2016 NDAA. I cannot emphasize enough how important maritime capacity-building is to our overarching strategy.

Third, we are leveraging defense diplomacy and building greater transparency. We are trying to reduce the risk of miscalculation or conflict and promoting shared maritime rules of the road. The Department is actively seeking to mitigate risk in maritime Asia both for bilateral efforts with China, as well as region-wide risk reduction measures.

These and other elements of United States-China defense diplomacy have yielded some positive results. United States and PLA [People's Liberation Army] Navy vessels have now successfully employed the code for unplanned encounters at sea on multiple occasions during recent interactions. I would note that while the United States operates consistent with the United Nations Convention on the Law of the Sea [UNCLOS], we have seen positive momentum in promoting shared rules of the road. Our efforts would be greatly strengthened by Senate ratification of UNCLOS. Mr. Chairman, I would like to thank you and other members for your support on this issue.

Finally, we are working to strengthen regional security institutions and encourage the development of an open and effective regional security architecture. ASEAN [Association of Southeast Asian Nations] is an increasingly important DOD partner, and the Department is enhancing its engagement in ASEAN-based institutions. This includes efforts such as our decision to host ASEAN defense ministers for their 2014 U.S.-ASEAN Defense Forum, as well as Secretary Carter's recent announcement of DOD's commitment to deploy a technical advisor in support of ASEAN's maritime security efforts.

Throughout its history, the U.S. has relied upon and advocated for freedom of the seas. This freedom is essential to our economic and security interests and nowhere more so than in the Asia-Pacific. The Department is constantly working to evaluate the strategic environment to ensure we have the necessary strategy, resources, and tools to meet the challenges we face. We are clear-eyed about the growing complexity of this task. Yet, we are making progress that, over the long term, will be significant in shaping the regional security environment. We are making calculated and careful investments. We are gaining unprecedented access in the region. Our relationships and interoperability with allies and partners are stronger than ever before. Moreover, partners across the region are enhancing their defense cooperation with each other in unprecedented ways.

In short, we are deeply committed to the maritime security of the Asia-Pacific region. We do not discount the extent of the challenges, but we are undertaking a comprehensive effort to ensure that maritime Asia remains open, free, and secure in the decades ahead.

Thank you very much.

[The prepared statement of Secretary Shear follows:]

PREPARED STATEMENT BY HON. DAVID B. SHEAR

INTRODUCTION

Thank you very much Chairman McCain. Thank you also to Ranking Member Reed and other members of the committee for inviting me to be here to speak with you today.

I am pleased to be here to discuss maritime issues in the Asia-Pacific and the Department of Defense's new Asia-Pacific Maritime Security Strategy, which we released last month. This strategy reflects the enduring interests the United States has in the region and the premium we place on maritime peace and security in this critical part of the world. Throughout its history, the United States has relied upon and advocated for freedom of the seas, and this freedom is essential to our economic and security interests, nowhere more so than in the Asia-Pacific.

It is important to note that while this strategy reflects the Defense Department's maritime objectives and activities in the Asia-Pacific, DOD's efforts are simply one aspect of a much broader U.S. strategy to protect America's principled interests in upholding international law, freedom of navigation, unimpeded lawful commerce, and peaceful resolution of disputes. The United States has a comprehensive strategy to uphold maritime security in the region—one that leverages diplomacy, multilateral institutions, commitment to international law, maritime capacity building, trade, and continued engagement across the region.

The Department of Defense plays an important part in supporting these goals. For seventy years, our robust maritime capabilities, and the presence of U.S. sailors, soldiers, Marines, and airmen, have helped protect the freedom of navigation and commerce upon which the United States and all Asia-Pacific nations rely. As we note in the Asia-Pacific Maritime Security Strategy report, "freedom of the seas" reflects far more than simply freedom of navigation for commercial vessels. It also implies all of the rights, freedoms, and lawful uses of the sea and airspace, including for military ships and aircraft, recognized under international law.

Unfortunately, in recent years, we have seen a number of changes take place in the maritime security environment that have the potential to undermine the freedoms and the peace and security the region has enjoyed for decades. So before I discuss the details of our strategy, allow me to offer some thoughts on the strategic context for this report.

STRATEGIC CONTEXT

Over the past several decades, the Asia-Pacific has experienced one of the most tremendous economic transformations in modern history, thanks in no small part to the growth of free and open trade across the region's sea lanes. As Secretary Carter noted, this growth has been the result of a peaceful security environment. While regional trade and prosperity continue to grow, recent developments in the maritime domain, if left unaddressed, could challenge the stable security environment that has enabled this historic progress. These include rapid military modernization, growing competition for resources, and intensifying territorial and maritime disputes.

In recent years, Asia-Pacific nations have significantly increased their surface, subsurface, and air capabilities, leading to a dramatic increase in the number of military planes and vessels operating in close proximity in the maritime domain. At the same time, this military modernization has been accompanied by a corresponding increase in regional law enforcement capabilities, which have become increasingly relevant as some countries, particularly China, are using their civilian assets to assert claims over disputed maritime areas.

While military modernization efforts are a natural and expected element of economic growth, they also increase the potential for dangerous miscalculations or conflict. This places a premium on the need for Asia-Pacific nations to adhere to shared maritime rules of the road, such as the Code for Unplanned Encounters at Sea (CUES), and to pursue increased transparency and risk reduction mechanisms to ensure safe behavior in the maritime domain.

The potential for instability is also exacerbated by the existence of long-standing territorial and maritime disputes across the region, most notably in the South China Sea. While we do not take a position on conflicting territorial claims in the South China Sea, we do emphasize that all maritime claims must be derived from land features in accordance with international law as reflected in the Law of the Sea Convention, and any disputes should be settled peacefully and in accordance with international law. We have called for all claimants to reciprocally and permanently halt land reclamation, the construction of new facilities, and the further militarization of outposts on disputed features. We have also encouraged all claimants to conclude a Code of Conduct by the time of the East Asia Summit in November, one that would create clear rules of the road in the South China Sea.

China's large-scale land reclamation on disputed features over the past two years has brought concerns about regional stability into sharper focus. While land reclamation is not a new development, and China is not the only claimant to have conducted reclamation, China's recent activities significantly exceed other efforts in size, pace, and effect. China has now reclaimed more than 2,900 acres, amounting to 17 times more land in 20 months than the other claimants combined over the past 40 years, and accounting for approximately 95 percent of all reclaimed land in the Spratly Islands. China has clearly stated that the outposts will have a military component to them, and by undertaking these actions, China is not only unilaterally altering the status quo in the region, they are also complicating the lowering of tensions and the resolution of South China Sea disputes. We continue to encourage all claimants to commit to reciprocally and permanently halt further land reclamation, construction, and militarization of outposts in the South China Sea, in order to create space for diplomatic solutions to emerge.

DOD'S MARITIME STRATEGY

The Department has devised a comprehensive and systematic maritime strategy to meet these challenges. Our strategy is focused on three fundamental goals: *safe-*

guarding the freedom of the seas; deterring conflict and coercion; and promoting adherence to international law and standards.

In pursuit of these goals, the Department is: strengthening United States military capacity; building the maritime capabilities of allies and partners in maritime Asia; reducing the risk of potential conflicts by leveraging military diplomacy; and strengthening regional security institutions.

Strengthening U.S. Military Capacity

As part of the rebalance to the Asia-Pacific, we are strengthening our military capacity to ensure the United States can successfully deter conflict and coercion and respond decisively when needed. To achieve this objective, the Department is investing in new cutting-edge capabilities, deploying our finest maritime capabilities forward, and distributing these capabilities more widely across the region.

We also are enhancing our regional force posture—particularly air and maritime assets—to ensure our ability to execute key missions. We are deploying some of our most advanced surface ships to the Asia-Pacific, including replacing the aircraft carrier *USS George Washington* in 2015 with the newer *USS Ronald Reagan;* sending our newest air operations-oriented amphibious assault ship, the *USS America,* to the region by 2020; deploying two additional Aegis-capable destroyers to Japan; and home-porting all three of our newest class of stealth destroyers, the DDG–1000, with the Pacific fleet. Through these and other efforts, the U.S. Navy will increase the size of Pacific Fleet's overseas assigned forces by approximately 30 percent over the next five years.

This enhanced military capacity will allow the Department to maintain a higher tempo of routine and persistent maritime presence activities across the Asia-Pacific. In short, you will see more of the U.S. Navy in the region in the coming years. United States Pacific Command maintains a robust shaping presence in and around the South China Sea, with activities ranging from training and exercises with allies and partners to port calls to Freedom of Navigation Operations and other routine operations. These activities are central to our efforts to dissuade conflict, preserve our access to the region, encourage peaceful resolution of maritime disputes and adherence to the rule of law, and to strengthen our relationships with partners and allies.

A key component of DOD operations falls under the Freedom of Navigation (FON) program, conducted in conjunction with our interagency partners. The Department is placing new emphasis on these operations, which challenge excessive maritime claims around the world and directly support adherence to international maritime law. Between 2013 and 2014, we increased *global FON operations* by 84 percent, the majority of which were conducted in the Asia-Pacific. As Secretary Carter has stated, the United States will continue to fly, sail, and operate wherever international law allows, as U.S. forces do all around the world, and our FON Operations are a critical example of this.

The Department is also enhancing its forward presence by using existing assets in new ways, across the entire region, with an emphasis on operational flexibility and maximizing the value of U.S. assets despite the tyranny of distance. This is why the Department is working to develop a more distributed, resilient, and sustainable posture. As part of this effort, the United States will maintain its presence in Northeast Asia, while enhancing defense posture across the Western Pacific, Southeast Asia, and the Indian Ocean. The cornerstone of our forward presence will continue to be our presence in Japan, and in an effort to ensure that this presence is sustainable, we have worked within the alliance to develop a new laydown for the U.S. Marine Corps in the Pacific. Through the bilateral Force Posture Agreement (FPA) with Australia and the Enhanced Defense Cooperation Agreement (EDCA) with the Philippines, the Department will be able to increase our routine and persistent rotational presence in Southeast Asia for expanded training with regional partners.

Through these efforts, there should be no doubt that the United States will maintain the necessary military presence and capabilities to protect our interests and those of our allies and partners against potential threats in the maritime domain.

Building Ally and Partner Capacity

However, our strategy involves far more than U.S. capacity and presence. The bedrock of our approach in the region is our strong network of allies and partners, and the combined capabilities these relationships can bring to bear. Through regular and close consultations with our allies and partners from Northeast Asia to the Indian Ocean, the Department of Defense is working to bolster the maritime capacity and capabilities of countries in the region.

First, we are building greater interoperability and developing more integrated operations with our allies and partners. For example, with our close ally Japan, we are working to improve the maritime-related capabilities of the Japan Self-Defense Forces. As Japan acquires advanced capabilities such as V–22 Ospreys, E–2D Hawkeyes, and Global Hawk Unmanned Aerial Vehicles, we are building a stronger and more interoperable alliance. Our expanded bilateral cooperation will now encompass a range of activities, from peacetime cooperation on shared maritime domain awareness, up to cooperation across a range of contingencies. In Southeast Asia, the Department is assisting the Philippines to more effectively establish a minimum credible defense, and we have established new bilateral working groups with Vietnam, Indonesia, and Singapore to support their maritime defense requirements. In South Asia, we are working with the Indian Navy on aircraft carrier technology sharing and design; the United States-India Joint Aircraft Carrier Working Group (JACWG) had its first formal meeting in August, led by Vice ADM Cheema, the Commander in Chief of India's Western Fleet.

We also are increasing the size, frequency, and sophistication of our regional exercise program, with a particular focus on developing new exercises with Southeast Asian partners and expanding our multilateral exercise program. A large contingent of United States, Philippine, and Australian military personnel participated in this year's exercise Balikatan in the Philippines, including observers from Japan. DOD is continuing to expand its maritime engagements elsewhere in Southeast Asia, with important partners like Indonesia, Malaysia, and Vietnam. In Indonesia, the April 2015 iteration of the Sea Surveillance Exercises included a flight portion over the South China Sea for the first time, and the United States Marine Corps participated in an amphibious exercise with the Malaysian Armed Forces. In Vietnam, we are rapidly growing our maritime training, and in just six years, our naval cooperation has grown from a simple port visit to multi-day engagements that allow our sailors to better understand each other's operations and procedures.

Our maritime capacity building efforts in Southeast Asia do not stop there. As Secretary Carter announced at the Shangri-La Dialogue, the Department is implementing a new Southeast Asia Maritime Security Initiative (MSI) that will increase training and exercises, personnel support, and maritime domain awareness capabilities for our partners in Southeast Asia. As part of MSI, DOD, in coordination with the Department of State, will consult with our allies and partners to define the requirements needed to accomplish the goals of MSI and explore other enduring opportunities for maritime collaboration. In the near term, we are focused on several lines of effort: working with partners to expand regional maritime domain awareness capabilities and develop a regional common operating picture; providing the necessary infrastructure, logistics support, and operational procedures to enable more effective maritime response operations; strengthening partner nation operational capabilities through expanded maritime exercises and engagements; helping partners strengthen their maritime institutions, governance, and personnel training; and identifying modernization and new system requirements for critical maritime security capabilities. I not only thank you for remaining focused on this important effort, but also urge your continued support as we move forward to implement this strategy.

Reducing Risk

In addition to our efforts to improve regional capabilities, the Department is also leveraging defense diplomacy to build greater transparency, reduce the risk of miscalculation or conflict, and promote shared maritime rules of the road. The Department is pursuing a two-pronged approach to achieve this objective, one focusing on our bilateral relationship with China, and the other focused on region-wide risk reduction measures.

In recent years, we have reinvigorated efforts to expand bilateral risk reduction mechanisms with China, including the Military Maritime Consultative Agreement (MMCA) and the establishment of an historic Memorandum of Understanding (MOU) on Rules of Behavior for Safety of Air and Maritime Encounters in 2014. This MOU established a common understanding of operational procedures for air and maritime encounters to reduce the possibility of misunderstanding between the United States and Chinese militaries. The MOU currently includes an annex on ship-to-ship encounters and we are working to expand it further by the end of 2015. Already, United States-China defense diplomacy has yielded positive results; there have been no unsafe intercepts since August 2014. In further efforts to reduce risk, U.S. Navy and PLA Navy vessels have successfully employed CUES during recent interactions, lowering the likelihood of miscalculations that could lead to dangerous escalation.

Of course, reaching agreement on bilateral risk reduction measures with China is necessary, but not sufficient. The Department is also working to help the Association of Southeast Asian Nations (ASEAN) and other regional partners establish regional risk reduction mechanisms, such as operational-level hotlines to establish more reliable and routine crisis communication mechanisms. As I mentioned, MSI will help develop a regional common operating picture to reduce risk, but we also encourage the efforts of countries that seek to reduce tensions through their own initiatives—such as Indonesia and Malaysia—who recently announced their intention to exchange maritime envoys in an effort to increase mutual transparency. We also have supported the efforts between China and Japan to do the same in the East China Sea.

Building Regional Architecture

Finally, we are working to strengthen regional security institutions and encourage the development of a transparent, integrated, and diversified effective regional security architecture. ASEAN is an increasingly important DOD partner, and the Department is continuing to enhance its engagement in ASEAN-based institutions such as the ASEAN Defense Ministers Meeting Plus (ADMM–Plus). To this end, Secretary Carter will travel to Kuala Lumpur in November for the next ADMM–Plus meeting. This will follow a host of new initiatives and engagements with various ASEAN-related institutions. For example, at the May 2015 Shangri-La Dialogue in Singapore, the Secretary of Defense announced DOD's commitment to deploy a technical advisor to augment the U.S. Mission to ASEAN in support of ASEAN's maritime security efforts, and we are making progress toward that goal. We are also leveraging informal opportunities to strengthen regional cooperation, such as the first United States-ASEAN Defense Forum then-Secretary of Defense Chuck Hagel hosted in Hawaii in April 2014. Through these venues, we aim to promote candid conversations about ongoing challenges in the maritime domain, and encourage greater information sharing and cooperative solutions.

At its core, any discussion about the future of the Asia-Pacific naturally involves a discussion about maritime security, given the defining characteristic of the maritime domain in the region. Our strategy enables countries in the region to have confidence in our conviction to uphold our principled maritime interests. Our strategy also is designed to strengthen the rules-based order, where laws and standards, not size and strength, determine outcomes to disputes. We are not alone in seeking to advance this vision for the region, which aligns our interests with our values; indeed, it is widely shared by countries across the region that eagerly support our efforts. Even as we address immediate challenges to our interests and those of our allies and partners, we remain committed to this longer term goal.

CONCLUSION

The Asia-Pacific and its maritime waterways remain critical to United States security. The Department is actively working to stay ahead of the evolving maritime security environment in the Asia-Pacific by implementing a comprehensive strategy that will protect peace and stability in the maritime domain. Together with our interagency colleagues and regional allies and partners, the Department will help ensure that maritime Asia remains open, free, and secure in the decades ahead.

Senator McCain. Thank you.
Admiral Harris?

STATEMENT OF ADMIRAL HARRY B. HARRIS, JR., USN, COMMANDER U.S. PACIFIC COMMAND

Admiral Harris. Thank you, Chairman McCain, Senator Reed, and distinguished members. It is my honor to appear once again before this committee. I am pleased to be here with Assistant Secretary Shear to discuss the Asia-Pacific maritime strategies.

The United States is a maritime nation and the importance of the Asia-Pacific region to our Nation's security and prosperity cannot be overstated. Almost 30 percent of the world's maritime trade, as the chairman said, over $5 trillion, transits the South China Sea annually. This includes $1.2 trillion in ship-borne trade bound for the United States. The Asia-Pacific region is critical for our Nation's economic future.

For decades, this region has remained free from major conflicts, allowing the United States and other Pacific nations, including

China, to enjoy the benefits of its vast maritime spaces. However, the security environment is changing, potentially placing this stability at risk. Rapid economic and military modernization and a growing demand for resources have increased the potential for conflict. Peacetime freedom of navigation is under pressure.

If not handled properly, territorial and maritime disputes in the East and South China Seas could disrupt stability throughout the region. Claimants to disputed areas routinely use maritime law enforcement and coast guard vessels to enforce their claims while nominally keeping these issues out of the military sphere. While no country appears to desire military conflict, tactical miscalculations can lead to strategic consequences.

The United States does not take sides on issues of sovereignty with respect to these territorial disputes, but we do insist that all maritime claims be derived from naturally-formed land features in accordance with customary international law, as reflected in the Law of the Sea Convention. The United States also emphasizes the importance of peacefully resolving maritime and territorial disagreements in accordance with international law, and we oppose the use of intimidation, coercion, or aggression. The U.S. believes every nation, large or small, should have the opportunity to develop and prosper in line with international laws and standards. If one country selectively ignores these rules for its own benefit, others will undoubtedly follow, eroding the international legal system and destabilizing regional security and the prosperity of all Pacific states. Part of PACOM's [United States Pacific Command] role in the Asia-Pacific maritime strategy will be ensuring all nations have continued access to the maritime spaces vital to the global economy.

International recognition and protection of freedom of navigation is vital to the world's economy and our way of life. To safeguard the freedom of the seas, PACOM routinely exercises with allies and partners, executes freedom of navigation operations, and maintains a robust presence throughout the region. These activities help build partner capacity to contribute to the region's stability, enhance relationships, improve understanding of shared challenges, and message the U.S.'s resolve.

The Asia-Pacific maritime security strategy outlines our plan to safeguard freedom of the seas, deter conflict, and promote adherence to international laws and standards. It reaffirms our commitment to the principles found in UNCLOS, and in accordance with this strategy and in pursuit of these goals, Pacific Command's forces fly, sail, and operate wherever international law allows, while continuing to strengthen the relationships and rule of law that enabled the peaceful rise of every nation in the region.

A fundamental factor in the feasibility of this new strategy has been the rebalance to the Pacific. The rebalance, initiated almost 4 years ago by President Obama, set the conditions for the implementation of this strategy. The rebalance strengthened treaty alliances and partnerships, increased partner capacities and cooperation, improved interoperability, and increased security capabilities in the region. DOD's new maritime strategy capitalizes on the momentum of the rebalance and continues with its initiatives.

In executing the new maritime strategy, PACOM will continue to employ the most advanced and capable platforms as they are deployed or assigned to the Pacific; use the forward presence of military forces to engage allies and partners to deter aggression; reinforce internationally accepted rules and norms, including the concepts of freedom of navigation and innocent passage; train and exercise with allies and partners to increase interoperability and build trust; implement risk reduction mechanisms such as the Code for Unplanned Encounters at Sea and the United States-China Confidence Building Measures to help prevent accidents and tactical miscalculations; and continue deepening alliances and partnerships through strategic efforts in places like Japan, Korea, Australia, Thailand, and the Philippines, while building new and deeper relationships in places like Singapore, India, Vietnam, and other likeminded friends and partners.

Thank you for your continued support to USPACOM and our men and women in uniform and their families who live and work in the vast Asia-Pacific region. I look forward to answering your questions.

[The prepared statement of Admiral Harris follows:]

PREPARED STATEMENT BY ADMIRAL HARRY B. HARRIS, JR.

Chairman McCain, Senator Reed, and distinguished members, it's my honor to appear once again before this committee. I am pleased to be here with Assistant Secretary Shear to discuss the Asia Pacific Maritime Security Strategy.

The United States is a maritime nation and the importance of Asia-Pacific region to our Nation's security and prosperity cannot be overstated. Almost 30 percent of the world's maritime trade—$5.3 trillion—transits the South China Sea annually. This includes $1.2 trillion in ship-borne trade bound for the United States. The Asia-Pacific region is critical for our nation's economic future.

For decades, this region has remained free from major conflicts, allowing the United States and other Pacific nations, including China, to enjoy the benefits of its vast maritime spaces. However, the security environment is changing, potentially placing this stability at risk. Rapid economic and military modernization and a growing demand for resources have increased the potential for conflict. Peacetime freedom of navigation is under pressure.

If not handled properly, territorial and maritime disputes in the East and South China Seas could disrupt stability throughout the region. Claimants to disputed areas routinely use maritime law enforcement and coast guard vessels to enforce their claims while nominally keeping these issues out of the military sphere. While no country appears to desire military conflict, tactical miscalculations can lead to strategic consequences.

The United States does not take sides on issues of sovereignty with respect to these territorial disputes, but we do insist that all maritime claims be derived from naturally-formed land features in accordance with customary international law, as reflected in the Law of the Sea Convention. The United States also emphasizes the importance of peacefully resolving maritime and territorial disagreements in accordance with international law, and we oppose the use of intimidation, coercion, or aggression. The U.S. believes every nation, large or small, should have the opportunity to develop and prosper, in line with international laws and standards. If one country selectively ignores these rules for its own benefit, others will undoubtedly follow, eroding the international legal system and destabilizing regional security and the prosperity of all Pacific states. Part of PACOM's role in the Asia-Pacific Maritime Strategy will be ensuring all nations have continued access to the maritime spaces vital to the global economy.

International recognition and protection of freedom of navigation is vital to the world's economy and our way of life. To safeguard the freedom of the seas, USPACOM routinely exercises with allies and partners, executes Freedom of Navigation operations, and maintains a robust presence throughout the region. These activities help build partner capacity to contribute to the region's security, enhance relationships, improve understanding of shared challenges, and message the U.S.'s resolve.

The Asia-Pacific Maritime Security Strategy outlines our plan to safeguard freedom of the seas, deter conflict, and promote adherence to international law and standards. It reaffirms our commitment to the principles found in UNCLOS. In accordance with this strategy and in pursuit of these goals, Pacific Command's forces will fly, sail, and operate wherever international law allows, while continuing to strengthen the relationships and rule of law that enabled the peaceful rise of every nation in the region.

A fundamental factor in the feasibility of this new strategy has been the Rebalance to the Pacific. The Rebalance, initiated almost four years ago by President Obama, set the conditions for the implementation of this strategy. The Rebalance strengthened treaty alliances and partnerships, increased partner capacity and co-operation, improved interoperability, and increased security capabilities in the region. DOD's new maritime strategy capitalizes on the momentum of the Rebalance and continues with its initiatives. In executing the new maritime strategy, PACOM will continue to:

- Employ the most advanced and capable platforms as they are deployed or assigned to the Pacific.
- Use the forward presence of military forces to engage allies and partners and deter aggression.
- Reinforce internationally accepted rules and norms including the concepts of freedom of navigation and innocent passage.
- Train and exercise with allies and partners to increase interoperability and build trust.
- Implement risk reduction mechanisms such as the Code for Unplanned Encounters at Sea and the United States-China Confidence Building Measures to help prevent accidents and tactical miscalculations.
- Continue deepening alliances and partnerships through strategic efforts in places like Japan, Korea, Australia, Thailand and the Philippines, while building new and deeper military relationships in places like Singapore, India, Vietnam, and with other like-minded friends and partners.

Thank you for your continued support to USPACOM and our men and women in uniform, and their families, who live and work in the vast Asia-Pacific region. I look forward to answering your questions.

Senator McCAIN. Well, thank you, Admiral.

Maybe I can begin with this news report out of Defense One, Defiant Chinese Admiral's Message: South China Sea Belongs to China. There was a gathering I think in London, and there was Chinese and American and Japanese, as well as other military leaders. The admiral who commands the North Sea fleet for the People's Liberation Army and Navy, South China Sea is the name indicated as a sea area. It belongs to China.

What is our response to that, Mr. Secretary?

Secretary SHEAR. Thank you, Senator.

The Chinese have said that before. It was nothing new for the admiral to have said that. If he was referring to the area of the South China Sea demarcated by the so-called nine-dash line, it is clear to us that that nine-dash line is not consistent with international law, and we do not recognize the Chinese claim to the area encompassed by the nine-dash line.

With regard to our operations in that area, we sail and we fly and we operate within that area on a daily basis. Every time we do so——

Senator McCAIN. You operate within that area, but you have not operated within 12 miles of these reclaimed features. Have you?

Secretary SHEAR. We have conducted freedom of navigation operations.

Senator McCAIN. Have we gone within the 12 miles of the reclaimed area? The answer I believe is no.

Secretary SHEAR. We have not recently gone within 12 miles of a reclaimed area. However——

Senator MCCAIN. When was the last time we did?

Secretary SHEAR. I believe the last time we conducted a freedom of navigation operation in the South China Sea was April of this year.

Senator MCCAIN. Within the 12-mile limit. Come on, Mr. Secretary. I am very interested in the 12-mile limit because if you respect the 12-mile limit, then that is de facto sovereignty agreed to tacitly to the Chinese.

Now, have we or have we not operated within the 12-mile limit in recent years?

Secretary SHEAR. I believe the last time we conducted a freedom of navigation operation within 12 nautical miles of one of those features was 2012.

Senator MCCAIN. 2012, 3 years ago.

Secretary SHEAR. I might add, Senator, if I may, that freedom of navigation operations are one tool in a larger toolbox that we are going to need to use in fixing this issue. We are in the process of putting together that toolbox. As we move forward, we are going to consider freedom of navigation operations, along with a variety of other options to ensure that both the Chinese and the region understands that we can operate and we do operate anywhere we can.

Senator MCCAIN. Then it seems to me that we ought to do it because you see the area that has now been filled in. Since the last time we operated within the 12-mile limit, that number of acres has been dramatically increased, and we have watched it and really—well, the best sign of respecting freedom of the seas is not to de facto recognize a 12-mile limit, and the best way you can make sure that that is not recognized is to sail your ships in international waters, which it clearly is—these are artificial islands—and pass right on by. That then puts the lie to the admiral who said the South China Sea is—he indicated it belongs to China. It does not belong to China. It belongs to the international waterways. If people are allowed to fill in islands and so, therefore, then they are subject to a 12-mile limit. The best way to prove that they are not is to go ahead and go in it. We have not done that since 2012. I do not find that acceptable, Mr. Secretary. With all the other tools you have in the toolbox, the most visible assertion of freedom of the seas is to peacefully sail inside the 12-mile limit of artificial islands, which in any version of international law is not allowed to be sovereign territory of any nation.

Secretary SHEAR. Well, I agree with you, Mr. Chairman, that the South China Sea does not belong to China. We have in recent years conducted freedom of navigation operations in the vicinity of those features, and doing so again is one of the array of options we are considering.

Senator MCCAIN. Well, it is an option that has not been exercised in 3 years.

Spratly Islands Reclamation Comparison
(Each Flag Represents 10 acres)

China (2,900 acres)

Vietnam (80 acres)
Malaysia (70 acres)
The Philippines (14 acres)
Taiwan (8 acres)

Source: DOD, Asia-Pacific Maritime Security Strategy, August 2015

15

Admiral Harris, what do you feel about it?

Admiral HARRIS. Sir, I agree that the South China Sea is no more China's than the Gulf of Mexico is Mexico's. I think that we must exercise our freedom of navigation throughout the region. Part of my responsibility as the Pacific Command Commander is to give options to the President and to the Secretary, and those options are being considered and we will execute as directed by the President and the Secretary.

Senator MCCAIN. I have gone over my time, but just very quickly, Mr. Secretary, with respect to China, do you agree with DNI [Director of National Intelligence] Clapper's comments that the United States has no effective policy to deter China in cyberspace? Last week, he testified before the House Intelligence Committee. The United States lacked, quote, both the substance and the mindset of deterrence in cyberspace.

Secretary SHEAR. I would refer to what the President said last Friday when he stated that we can have a competition in cyberspace with China or with other countries, but we will win. What we are seeking is understandings.

Senator MCCAIN. Are we winning now?

Secretary SHEAR. I agree with General Clapper that deterring actions in cyberspace is very difficult.

Senator MCCAIN. Are we winning now?

Secretary SHEAR. I think everybody knows that we have the capability to——

Senator MCCAIN. You know, Mr. Secretary, we have known each other a long time. I mean, are we winning now in your view?

Secretary SHEAR. I think it is too early to tell, Mr. Chairman. We are doing our best.

Senator MCCAIN. Thank you.

Senator Reed?

Senator REED. Well, thank you very much, Mr. Chairman.

Just to clarify the type of operations, have we conducted flyovers of these artificial facilities recently? When is the most recent flyover?

Secretary SHEAR. I defer to the Admiral on that question, sir.

Admiral HARRIS. Senator Reed, we have not conducted a flyover—a direct flyover—overfly of any of the reclaimed lands and territories that China has reclaimed recently.

Senator REED. That is another option that you have, but you have not exercised that option.

Admiral HARRIS. You are correct, sir. We have a lot of options that are on the table.

Senator REED. Mr. Secretary, just stepping back a bit, one of the things that is happening in China now is extraordinary economic volatility, growth rates that are being challenged, which if you have an insight, if you do not, then let me know. This economic—and it may be long-term. It may be just something that is cyclic. Is it encouraging them or discouraging them when it comes to these policies in the South China Sea? Your insight. Is it something that—you know, they felt several years ago that they had sort of turned the corner, that their economic power was so great that they could begin to move forward. Are any of those questions being raised internally now in China about their capacity? Or the alternative would be are they going to double down because they have had economic problems at home, and therefore, we can expect them to be even more provocative? Any insights.

Secretary SHEAR. Those are all extremely relevant questions, Senator. I am not an economist and I am not an expert on the Chinese economy, but I think to the extent that the Communist Party relies on economic performance for its legitimacy, then I would suspect it is very concerned about recent overall economic performance. I think we have to be alert to the possibility that the Chinese might use a problem in foreign affairs to distract people's attention from their domestic problems.

On the subject of Chinese assertiveness, I think it is only natural for a country like China that is growing in wealth to turn to military modernization. I think Chinese military modernization and the growth of their defense budget has been extremely robust. We remain very concerned about the pace of growth in the Chinese defense budget and the lack of transparency and the overall effect that has on regional stability. Of course, as they modernize, one would expect them to become more assertive abroad, and that is just what we are doing and that is something that we are addressing with this regional security strategy.

Senator REED. Admiral Harris, as I indicated in my opening remarks, there is concern about North Korea. In fact, I recall when we met in Singapore, you expressed significant concern. Can you just briefly give us your latest update about North Korean activities? Also I might add since China shares a border with North Korea, are they at all being helpful or do they recognize the threats that are posed by the regime in North Korea?

Admiral HARRIS. Senator, I believe, as I have said before, that North Korea is the greatest threat that I face in the Pacific as a Pacific Command commander. I think that you have a leader in North Korea who has nuclear weapons and is seeking the means to miniaturize them and deliver them intercontinentally, and that causes me great concern. He has got 20,000 to 30,000 artillery pieces within a range of Seoul, amounting to several hundred thousand rockets that place the 28,000 American troops plus their families and the 700,000 American citizens who live on the Korean peninsula in danger. So I view the threat from North Korea very seriously.

I think that China's influence on North Korea is waning, or China does not have the influence on North Korea that it had in the past. So that is also an area of concern. There are many areas globally where we cooperate with China, and one of the areas in the past where we have received cooperation from China has been to mitigate the behavior of North Korea. We are not seeing that today. That causes me great concern.

Senator REED. So one of the initiatives that we have with the Chinese is not just checking their disregard for international law of the sea, et cetera, but also reengaging them to work together to face a very significant threat in North Korea. Is that accurate?

Admiral HARRIS. You are correct, sir. I have been very critical of Chinese behavior in the last 2 years, but I have also been—I have acknowledged where China has been helpful. They have been helpful in removal of chemical weapons from Syria, in the counter-piracy efforts off the Horn of Africa, and the search for the Malaysia airliner MH370 off of Australia, and the support to the Philippines in the November 2013 typhoon that hit that country. So we should acknowledge those good things that China has done. At the same time, I would be critical and hold them to account for those negative things they do.

Senator REED. Mr. Secretary, do you have a quick comment?

Secretary SHEAR. Sir, if I may add to that. We exchange views with the Chinese on North Korea regularly. I did so in Beijing with my Chinese PLA counterparts just 10 days ago. The Chinese reiterated to me, as they have in the past, that their influence with North Korea is limited, particularly under the new regime. During the recent crisis related to the North Korean provocation on August 4, it was not clear to us that the Chinese had a lot of contact with the North Koreans or were able to significantly influence them.

Senator REED. Are they worried about that?

Secretary SHEAR. I think they are.

Senator REED. Thank you.

Senator MCCAIN. Senator Inhofe?

Senator INHOFE. Thank you, Mr. Chairman.

Let us talk about assets, current and future. Admiral Harris, one of the DOD lines of effort in our Asia-Pacific maritime security strategy says by 2020, 60 percent of naval and overseas air assets will be home-ported in the Pacific region. Okay?

Now, when you say that, right now in terms of our vessels, we have a fleet of 270. It should be 305. You are projecting now saying 60 percent of what it will be in 2020. What kind of figures are you looking at in calculating that?

Admiral HARRIS. Senator, the numbers you cited are correct. We have in the 270 range now, and by 2020, we should have a little over 300 ships, around 310. So we are talking 60 percent of actually a larger number, not a smaller.

Senator INHOFE. A larger number that we would anticipate would be available by that time, and I hope you are right.

Now, the source of those have to come up through other commands. Is that correct? If you increase to 60 percent, you will have to be taking some assets away from EUCOM [United States European Command], CENTCOM [United States Central Command], and other commands. Correct?

Admiral HARRIS. Right. Those commands now have assigned naval forces. Only the Pacific has forces that are assigned to the Pacific Command.

Senator INHOFE. They are using those assets.

Admiral HARRIS. That is correct.

Senator INHOFE. Are you coordinating with those when you make these assumptions and predictions as to what we should be doing in 2020 with the combatant commanders?

Admiral HARRIS. Yes, sir. As I have said before, the world gets a vote. So activities in Russia or other places could draw assets away.

Senator INHOFE. Yes, I understand that.

Admiral HARRIS. 60 percent of the Navy's combatants will be based in the Pacific at large by 2020.

Senator INHOFE. Admiral Harris, you have been around for quite awhile. You might remember what I refer to, sometimes not too affectionately, the Battle of Vieques. At that time—that was during the Clinton-Gore administration. At that time, the only place that we could identify in the world for integrated training was the Island of Vieques. You might remember that we had this big fight right here in this room. I will never forget it. It was primarily driven by Vice President Gore to do away with the live range down there.

Now, interestingly enough, those things that we said were going to happen to Roosey Roads [Roosevelt Roads Naval Station] and other assets there became a reality, and now they are begging us to come back.

Nonetheless, the point I am making is I went all over the world looking for areas where you can have this kind of integrated training. Where are we today in terms of our areas that we have available to us for the type of training that you have to have?

Admiral HARRIS. Senator, in the Pacific, we have integrated ranges. In Hawaii, the Pacific missile range facility is one of the finest in the world. In Guam. We are building new range facilities in the Guam operating area. These ranges, as you said, are vital to our ability to train. We are working with the countries involved, the states involved, and environmentalists that are involved in order to do this in the right way to satisfy all of the constituencies that are there and get our training done.

Senator INHOFE. Okay. You talked, Secretary Shear, a little bit about some of our exercises that we have out there. RIMPAC [The Rim of the Pacific Exercise] is one of the big ones. 22 nations were involved in that, 49 surface ships, 67 marines, 2,200 aircraft, some 25,000 personnel. It is a great exercise. I understand that. Do we have the assets now to continue that type of exercise for the near future?

Secretary SHEAR. I believe we do, sir. You are absolutely right that RIMPAC is a vital and important exercise not only for the U.S. but for the region. We believe we have the resources we need to continue conducting that.

Senator INHOFE. Well, I would hope that would be the case.

Thank you very much, Mr. Chairman.

Senator MCCAIN. Senator Shaheen?

Senator SHAHEEN. Thank you, Mr. Chairman.

Thank you both for testifying today.

Admiral Harris, in your testimony, you point out that we insist that all maritime claims be derived from naturally formed land features in accordance with international laws reflected in the Law of the Sea Convention. Are we in any kind of a disadvantage because we have not been a signatory to the Law of the Sea Convention?

Admiral HARRIS. Senator, I believe we are at a disadvantage because we do not have the moral high ground that other countries who are signatories, including China and Russia, have. So when China makes these outrageous claims in the South China Sea, and the Philippines, for example, challenges one of those claims in the international tribunal for Law of the Sea, and we support the Philippines right to make that claim, at the same time we are not a signatory. So that looks kind of strange.

When Russia makes these outrageous claims in the Arctic region in the Arctic Circle, and they tell us you have no standing on which to complain because you are not a signatory to the Law of the Sea, it puts us at a disadvantage.

Senator SHAHEEN. Thank you. I certainly agree. I would hope that we would reevaluate our position and become a signatory with most of the rest of the world of the Law of the Sea Convention.

Senator Reed raised the threat from North Korea. Secretary Shear, earlier this year, Admiral Gortney assessed that North Korea has the ability to launch an intercontinental ballistic missile that could be capable of hitting the United States from a mobile launcher, and we saw right before Secretary Carter visited Japan that they launched two short-range missiles. You talk about China and their waning influence with North Korea. Are there other measures that we ought to be taking with respect to North Korea? Should we have any sense of optimism about the recent overtures between North and South Korea where they seem to be talking a little more?

Secretary SHEAR. Thank you, Senator. That is an important question.

We certainly support the efforts by the North and South to conduct senior-level dialogue. As with past efforts to conduct such dialogue, I think we need to be very cautions in how we view the prospects. I view this current effort to be a direct outcome of the very robust position the ROK took in negotiations with the North at Panmunjom to resolve the issue precipitated by the North Korean provocation of August 4th. So I think it is very important that they have embarked on this effort, but we are just going to have to be very cautious. We support the ROK very strongly in these effort.

More generally, our approach to North Korea is a combination of diplomacy and pressure, and as we go forward toward a possible North Korean missile launch, for example, we are going to be engaging our Six Party partners, and we are going to be considering what extra pressure we might put on North Korea should they decide to conduct that missile launch.

Senator SHAHEEN. I assume you do not want to talk publicly about what those additional pressures might be?

Secretary SHEAR. Well, we put a great many sanctions on North Korea, and further sanctions would be one possibility.

Senator SHAHEEN. Did you want to add anything, Admiral Harris?

Admiral HARRIS. Sure, Senator. I will just add that I think the key is to be ready for all outcomes regarding North Korea from a position of strength. So I tend to be a pessimist when it comes to dealing with the capabilities of other countries. So, again, it is best to be cognizant of all outcomes, and that is why things like ballistic missile defense are important and we strengthen South Korea's ability in their BMD [Ballistic Missile Defence] systems. I personally believe the THAAD [Terminal High Altitude Area Defense] on the peninsula is important as well, the terminal high altitude missile defense system.

Senator SHAHEEN. There has been a lot of discussion today and earlier this year. Admiral Roughead, for example, noted that for the last decade, the United States has flown with impunity in Iraq and Afghanistan with no threat to anti-air weapons. He noted that our capabilities to do that will be threatened in the future as China has been able to field more capabilities.

I guess I would first say do you agree with that assessment. Then can you talk about what that new technology that China is developing and our ability to stay ahead—how that is going to be affected by sequestration? I do not know which one of you wants to——

Admiral HARRIS. Well, I will start. China fields a very modern military and they are growing in capability and capacity. We have a technological edge over them in almost every way, if not in every way. I am confident in our ability to take the fight to China, if it should come to that, and I certainly hope it does not.

That said, we have to maintain that technological edge, and they are growing in their technological capability and that is of concern to me. I think we need to have fifth generation fighters, for example, and we need to have a lot of them. That is the Joint Strike Fighter, the F–35. We need to continue to upgrade our fourth generation fighters with fifth generation capabilities because we have a lot of them, and I think that is important.

Senator SHAHEEN. Secretary Shear, I know I am out of time, but you just may want to add what you think, if cuts go back into effect for fiscal year 2016, what that would do to our ability to continue to have that technology.

Secretary SHEAR. Well, we are certainly concerned about the possible effects cuts may have both on current operations and our ability to develop the new technologies we need to maintain our military dominance in the region. That is something that Secretary Carter is extremely interested in. Our defense innovation initiative is designed to develop those capabilities we are going to need to counter area access and denial strategies and to maintain our security already in the region. So we are committed not only to deploying our best capabilities to the region now, we are committed to devising the technologies we need to maintain our edge.

Senator SHAHEEN. Thank you.

Thank you, Mr. Chairman.

Senator MCCAIN. Senator Ernst?

Senator ERNST. Thank you, Mr. Chair.

Thank you, gentlemen, for being here today. We appreciate it very much.

It was reported earlier this week that Japan will be providing $832 million in infrastructure aid to Vietnam and another $1.7 million worth of ships and equipment to them as well to help counter the rising of China. So I am very glad that our allies are improving their relationships to counter the Chinese aggression. Both Japan and Vietnam are key allies for us here in the United States, and developing that strong security and economic partnership with both Japan and Vietnam will allow us to better check China's aggression in that region.

So for both of you, if you would, please, how will this new agreement between Vietnam and Japan improve that security situation in that region and also, under the Southeast Asia Maritime Security Initiative, what specifically is the Department doing to build partner capacity and capability in Vietnam and in other Southeast Asia nations?

Secretary SHEAR. Thank you, Senator. That is a great point.

We strongly support Japanese efforts to coordinate with us in building partner capacity, particularly with countries like Vietnam, the Philippines, and probably in the future Malaysia. This is something that I worked on with my Japanese colleagues while I was Ambass ador in Hanoi, and I am delighted to see that it has come to fruition for the Japanese side.

We are interested in taking similar actions, as you state, in our maritime security initiative which is in the fiscal year 2016 NDAA. That is a 5-year, $425 million program, and we greatly appreciate the committee's support on this effort. Under that initiative, we hope to not only improve physical capacity of our partners in, say, providing, for example, coast guard vessels, but we want to improve their institutional capacity. We want to improve their sustainability, and that is something very important with the Philippines. We want to improve their professionalism. So this would be a very broad program designed to raise the level particularly of the maritime law enforcement capabilities of our partners in the region.

Admiral HARRIS. Senator, I was in Vietnam in my previous assignment as the Pacific Fleet commander, and I just returned from the Philippines a few weeks ago.

I welcome Japan's overtures and their efforts to improve the capacity of both countries, Vietnam and the Philippines. I think Vietnam presents an ideal opportunity for us as we work more closely with them. I think that that is another indication of the response of the region to China's bad behavior in the South China Sea where countries that previously were at odds with us or actually leaders of the Non-Aligned Movement are now coming to us for assistance and are opening themselves up to us. That is one of the costs that China has to bear for its bad behavior in the South China Sea region.

Senator ERNST. Very good. Thank you.

You have mentioned, both of you, the Philippines several times, and they have proven to be a great ally, whether it is the Global War on Terror, hurricane humanitarian relief efforts, and so forth. Are there specific steps that we can take or should be taking with the Philippines at this time to further develop those relationships?

Secretary SHEAR. You are right, Senator. More can be done. When the President was in Manila last year, he stated publicly that our commitment under the Mutual Defense Treaty to the Philippines is ironclad, that no one should have any doubt about the extent of our commitment under that treaty. We are working with the Philippines both in terms of—we are already working with the Philippines, even before we implement the maritime security initiative, to increase their capabilities to train and operate with them and to overall strengthen their ability to resist Chinese coercion.

Senator ERNST. Thank you, gentlemen, very much.

Thank you, Mr. Chair.

Senator MCCAIN. Senator Hirono?

Senator HIRONO. Thank you, Mr. Chairman.

Thank you, gentlemen. Admiral Harris, thank you so much for the briefing you gave me last month in Honolulu.

You mentioned, Admiral, that North Korea is the greatest threat that you face as Pacific Commander, and you noted that China's influence in North Korea is waning. Is there another country, i.e., Russia, that is stepping into this vacuum in relationships with North Korea?

Admiral HARRIS. Senator, I do not know of any Russian overtures with North Korea other than what I have read in open sources where they have always had some relationships with them because of their histories.

I believe that today the greatest threat I face is North Korea. North Korea today in my opinion is not an existential threat to the United States as Russia is. In the Pacific, as you know well, Russia has a long coastline. They have at least two major naval bases, including one for their ballistic missile submarines, two major air bases, and then a host of smaller operating bases in the Pacific. So these are things that I worry about as I look at the panoply of threats that the United States faces in the Pacific.

Senator HIRONO. Secretary Shear, we read recently that the Russians have recently approved significant infrastructure projects in what the Japanese call the "Northern Territories." There have been numerous visits to these remote locations by Russian leaders. So they are becoming active in that part of the world, not to mention in the Arctic.

I do share the concern that Admiral Harris raised that we are at a disadvantage by not being signatories to the Law of the Sea. Would you share that assessment?

Secretary SHEAR. I agree with you, Senator, on the importance of ratification of the Law of the Sea. I agree with the Admiral on his assessment of Russian activities in the Asia-Pacific. Let me stress that our maritime strategy is designed to encompass Russia, as well as China, as well as other challenges in the region.

Senator HIRONO. What do you make of Russia's activities in the Northern Territories? Is this for our domestic consumption, or does it have further reaching consequences?

Secretary SHEAR. Well, I confess, Senator, that I am not familiar with all the details on the kinds of infrastructure that Russia is building in the Northern Territories, but we support the Japanese claim to the Northern Territories. We would be concerned if the Russians used this infrastructure to further militarize or to bolster their military strength in the region.

Senator HIRONO. Admiral Harris, I was in Okinawa last month because, of course, part of the Indo-Asia-Pacific rebalance to this part of the world involves closing our Futenma facility. Most recently on Monday, Governor Onaga of Okinawa Prefecture proclaimed the he will proceed with canceling the landfill permit required for developing the alternative facility in Henoko. So for both of you, what does this proclamation mean for the Government of Japan and the Futenma replacement facility project that we need to get on with?

Admiral HARRIS. Senator, we have a longstanding treaty, mutual security treaty, with Japan. Our obligation in that treaty is to provide the security for Japan. One of Japan's obligations under that treaty is to provide us bases from which to operate and do that. Okinawa is critical to our ability to defend Japan and our posture in the Asia-Pacific region. It is a Japanese national effort and a decision whether to override or overcome Governor Onaga's objections to the Futenma replacement facility. They are working on that and I have confidence that they will achieve their national aims because that is their obligations under the treaty for us.

Secretary SHEAR. If I may add to that briefly, Senator. We greatly appreciate the support the Government of Japan has given to the effort to find a replacement for the Futenma facility. We appreciate their effort to get construction going for the Futenma replacement facility, and we were glad this week when we were informed by the Japanese Government that construction-related activities have begun at the Henoko site for the Futenma replacement facilities.

Senator HIRONO. So while there may be delays as a result of the Governor of Okinawa's actions, you expect that the Japanese Government will continue to proceed with the replacement facility.

Secretary SHEAR. I do, Senator. I want to stress that as we move forward on construction of the Futenma replacement facility, we, of course, as we always do, will continue to consider Okinawan sensitivities with regard to the general issue of our presence and our operations in Okinawa.

Senator HIRONO. Thank you.

Thank you, Mr. Chair.

Senator MCCAIN. Senator Lee?

Senator LEE. Thank you, Mr. Chairman.

Thank you, Admiral Harris and Secretary Shear, for all you do. Thanks for being here to answer our questions.

Admiral Harris, you have said that we need to ratify the Law of the Sea Treaty in order to acquire some type of moral high ground particularly relative to Russia and China. I am having a hard time seeing why it is that a country like the United States that has used its power, its blood, and its treasure to protect navigation all over the world for 200 years has to, in order to gain some moral high ground, ratify this particular treaty. Can you help me understand that?

Admiral HARRIS. Sure, Senator.

The lack of signing the treaty does not affect our ability to be the strongest nation on the earth, but the lack of signing that treaty puts us at a disadvantage in discussions with most of the other countries of the world that have signed the treaty and moral standing, if you will. So we lose nothing by signing off on the treaty, but we lose a lot by not signing it.

Senator LEE. What is the ''it'' that we lose? Part of what I would ask in connection with that, you know, one of the claims is that it might help us solve the South China Sea territorial disputes. All the nations in the South China Sea, including China, that have coastline along the South China Sea are members of the treaty. They are all parties to the treaty. The Philippines has brought a lawsuit against China under the treaty, and China, as I understand it, has basically ignored it. So how does that mean that this fixes the problem if we suddenly ratify the treaty?

Admiral HARRIS. Well, I do not think it would suddenly fix the problem, but as you said, the Philippines has brought a case against China in The Hague in the International Tribunal for Law of the Sea on two issues: one, on the veracity of the nine-dash line claim itself. Then the second issue is whether the tribunal has jurisdiction to even judge that case. We have supported the Philippines? right to take the claim to the international tribunal, and in fact, we have praised them for doing so. Yet, we are not a signatory to the treaty itself.

If you shift to the Arctic, if you look at the outrageous claims that Russia has made in the Arctic Ocean, they are making those claims under their interpretation of the Law of the Sea Convention. When we criticize them for those claims, they say that we have no standing to do so. I would submit that most of the rest of the world, who also has signed off on the treaty, would probably share that opinion or at least part of it.

On the other side, we have agreed as a policy to follow the precepts in the United Nations Convention on the Law of the Sea. So we have that for us, but we are not a signatory to it.

Again, I would say that in my opinion we lose nothing by signing it and we lose a lot of moral high groundedness, if you will, by not signing it.

Senator LEE. If we are following the precepts in the treaty, notwithstanding the fact that we have not ratified it and we, therefore, are not formally a party to it, I struggle with how that changes the moral high ground, particularly when I do not think there is any country on earth that has a greater claim to moral high ground, particularly when it comes to navigational issues, when it comes to naval issues, than the United States, which for 200 years has kept shipping lanes open and safe.

Can you tell me what navigational rights, if any, does the Navy lack today that it would suddenly have if we were to ratify that treaty?

Admiral HARRIS. Sir, the Navy would lack nothing whether we ratify the treaty or not. The United States would gain standing by signing off on the treaty.

Senator LEE. How would that standing benefit us in a material way relative to our interests in that part of the world?

Admiral HARRIS. Well, in some cases, under the—the convention sets up a framework for ocean exploration, for example, and it says that—we will not get into some of the real particulars—you go out to 200 miles and that is your exclusive economic zone, and then out beyond that is the open ocean zone, if you will. There are American companies today that will not explore out in that region beyond the 200-mile exclusive economic zone because they are not sure whether any competing claim will have an effect on them or whether they will lose in this international tribunal or other places. So I think that we lose an economic opportunity by not signing off on the treaty because it places in jeopardy the legal question, not the military or the strength question, but it places in jeopardy the legal question of what happens out beyond the exclusive economic zone. For our companies, they will gain an economic benefit from that.

Senator LEE. I see my time is expired.

I do not doubt the sincerity of your feelings on this. I would take issue with one aspect of what you said, though, that regardless of what benefits you might see from this, I would not say that signing onto a treaty is without any cost on our part without us giving up anything particularly, whereas here the treaty sets up a system that would, however incrementally, erode our national sovereignty.

Thank you, Mr. Chairman.

Senator McCain. Senator Nelson?

Senator Nelson. Gentlemen, thank you for your public service.

Admiral, where we have had the near misses in the 200- mile area that China is challenging us both in ships and in airplanes, we have successfully avoided those near misses where they have challenged us. Do you want to give us some insight into what your instructions are to our pilots and our ship captains with regard to those kind of incursions?

Admiral Harris. Sure, Senator. What I have told the component commanders, the Pacific fleet and Pacific air forces, to tell their pilots and crews to do is to continue to insist on our right to operate in international airspace and in maritime space. When challenged by Chinese fighter aircraft, our aircraft are to maintain professional flight profiles, predictable flight profiles, and we have means to record that activity and then we will see what happens. So the last time we saw a very dangerous event was in the middle of last year where the Chinese flew an aircraft over a P–8. They did a barrel roll over the top, which is a dangerous maneuver in acrobatic circles let alone in an intercept regime in the open ocean. We most recently have seen that again. I will give the system credit. For that intervening period of time, we have seen very few dangerous activities by the Chinese following that August 2014 incident. I think that is a tribute to the mil-to-mil relationship and the political relationship where we have worked with the Chinese to come to an agreement on the maritime and in the air spaces for confidence building measures.

Senator Nelson. Well, that is good news.

Now, is it going to be all the more strained given the 200-mile out from the China area? Now when you look at that map where they are filling in all of those islands and now they are claiming almost that entire ocean as theirs, are we going to see more and more of these incidents well beyond their 200-mile limit?

Admiral Harris. Certainly the potential exists for more incidents. If they finish building the airfields, of which there is one there on Fiery Cross Reef on the side and up to two additional airfields of 10,000-foot length, then that gives me great concern in the South China Sea. You know, if you look at National Airport, for example, National Airport is only 6,700 feet long, capable of landing any commercial airplane that we have, and China is building three runways of 10,000 foot length, which is only 1,000 foot shorter than would be required to land the Space Shuttle. So I think that that gives me great concern militarily.

They are also building deep water port facilities there, which could put their deep water ships, their combatant ships there, which gives them an extra capability.

If you look at all of these facilities and you can imagine a network of missile sites, runways for their fifth generation fighters and surveillance sites and all of that, it creates a mechanism by which China would have de facto control over the South China Sea in any scenario short of war. These are obviously easy targets in war. They will be what we call in the military "grapes," if you will. Short of that, they pose a—militarization of these features poses a threat, and certainly it poses a threat against all other countries in the region.

Senator NELSON. Speaking of those countries, to what degree are they vigorously stepping up with us to object to that kind of stuff?

Admiral HARRIS. Well, I think they are stepping up to the limits of their capabilities. So if you look at the Philippines, for example, they are doing it in probably the best way. They are taking it to an international tribunal for adjudication. I do not know how the tribunal is going to act or decide, and if they decide in the Philippines? favor, as Senator Lee said, I do not know if China is going to follow that. It puts China in a quandary if the international tribunal rules against China and China is a signatory to UNCLOS. So it gives the Philippines at least a moral high ground to make a claim.

The other countries are doing what they can also. You know, Chinese behavior in the South China Sea has enabled us to have a closer relationship with Vietnam, Indonesia, and Malaysia, and I think that is very important. Those are costs that China is having to expend because of its bad behavior in the South China Sea.

Secretary SHEAR. Sir, if I could just reinforce what the admiral just said. I, of course, share the admiral's concern about the military implications of Chinese activities in the South China Sea. That is why we are calling for a halt to further reclamation, a halt to construction, and a halt of further militarization of those facilities. The Chinese have not yet placed advanced weaponry on those features, and we are going to do everything we can to ensure that they do not. This is going to be a long-term effort. There are no silver bullets in this effort. We are certainly complicating Chinese calculations already.

If you pull back for a minute and look at our goals, which include safeguarding freedom of navigation and deterring coercion, I think we have made some gains in both these areas. We continue to operate freely in the South China Sea and we continue to prevent the Chinese from coercing our allies and partners into concluding deals that are not in their interests and not in our interests with regard to claims in the South China Sea.

Senator MCCAIN. That we freely operate in the South China Sea is a success? It is a pretty low bar, Mr. Secretary.

Senator Sullivan?

Senator SULLIVAN. Thank you, Mr. Chairman.

Thank you, gentlemen, for your service.

I think it is clear just from the testimony here and previous statements that we have a confused policy within the South China Sea with regard to the built-up islands. As you know, confusion can cause miscalculations. Let me just give you kind of the one example of it.

We were in Singapore for the Shangri-La Dialogue, the Secretary and Senator Reed, Senator Ernst, the chairman. Secretary Carter I thought had a forceful statement at the time. You know it, we have seen it. We will fly, sail anywhere. Then he stated, quote, after all, turning an underwater rock into an airfield simply does not afford the rights of sovereignty or permit restrictions on international air or maritime transport. A pretty strong statement in a very critical place.

Admiral Harris, you later stated I think at the Aspen Forum it is United States policy to afford a 12-mile limit around all the islands that are in the South China Sea, and it has been long-standing policy not because they are occupied or built up by China, but just in general. So to me that is a dramatic contrast. You have the PACOM Commander saying something very different than the Secretary of Defense. That is confusion.

We obviously have three policymaking centers going on here, the uniformed military, DOD civilians led by Secretary Carter, and the White House. In your professional opinion, Admiral Harris, should we sail or fly inside the 12-mile area with regard to those islands as Secretary Carter stated we should?

Admiral HARRIS. Senator, I believe that there is only one policy-making center, not three, and that runs through the Secretary of Defense and the President.

Senator SULLIVAN. No, but I am asking your professional opinion as a military——

Admiral HARRIS. I believe that we should exercise—be allowed to exercise freedom of navigation and maritime and flight in the South China Sea against those islands that are not islands.

Senator SULLIVAN. Inside the 12-mile limit.

Admiral HARRIS. Depending on the feature.

Senator SULLIVAN. What about that one?

Admiral HARRIS. That one, yes.

Senator SULLIVAN. Have you or Secretary Carter asked the White House for permission to do that?

Admiral HARRIS. Senator, I have given policy options—military options to the Secretary, and I would leave it to the Secretary or the Ambassador to address——

Senator SULLIVAN. What has the White House said when you have asked permission to go within the 12-mile zone of a feature like that?

Secretary SHEAR. Senator, PACOM, along with the Department of Defense, are options-generating institutions, and the Secretary is particularly interested in options with regard to the South China Sea in general.

Senator SULLIVAN. I just asked a simple question. What did the White House say if you asked for permission to go within inside the 12-mile limit? What did the White House say?

Secretary SHEAR. Conducting that kind of freedom of navigation operation is one of the operations we are considering.

Senator SULLIVAN. You are not answering my question. Did you ask the White House for permission to do this, and what did they tell you?

Secretary SHEAR. Sir, I am not able to discuss current policy deliberations, but I can assure you that that is one of the options that the administration is considering.

Senator SULLIVAN. Okay. I appreciate you just answering the question.

Secretary SHEAR. Again, I am just not able to go into the details of policy——

Senator SULLIVAN. Well, I think when the Secretary of Defense makes a definitive statement like that at a very important meeting of defense ministers in Asia and then we do not follow up on it, it undermines our credibility. That is something that we cannot afford anymore. Our credibility is undermined everywhere in the world, and we do it here.

It would be good if you could give me an answer to that question. You are obviously dodging it right now.

Secretary SHEAR. Sir, I would be delighted to give you the best possible answer, and I think that is that I am just not able to——

Senator SULLIVAN. I want to turn real quick to the Alaska incident that the chairman mentioned. I thought our reaction was almost—it was immediate. It was muted. It was almost apologetic relative to the way the Chinese respond when we come within 12 miles of one of their islands.

The President of the United States was in Alaska at the time. Do you believe that that was a coincidence that he was there, or do you believe that was a provocation that the Chinese were aggressively off the coast of Alaska when the President of the United States was visiting?

Secretary SHEAR. Well, I am not in a position to describe Chinese thinking on this, but——

Senator SULLIVAN. What is our analysis, either of you, from your perspective?

Admiral HARRIS. Senator, they were conducting an exercise with the Russians in the northern Pacific. I believe—my opinion—is they went into the Bering Sea to demonstrate their capability to operate that far north, and then they decided to go home.

Senator SULLIVAN. Do you think it was timed to coincide with the President of the United States——

Admiral HARRIS. No, I do not think it was—my opinion. I mean, I am not going into any intelligence matters at all. They were having an exercise with the Russians, and I think that exercise was long-planned. Then they decided to go into the Bering Sea. They were near there anyway. Then they turned south and headed home. I think it was coincidental, but I do not know that for a fact. Their transit south was an expeditious transit, innocent passage through two Aleutian Islands. That is their right to do under international law, as is our right to do in international law wherever we operate.

Senator SULLIVAN. Thank you.

Mr. Chairman, I thought it was more of a provocation and a demonstration of their interest in the Arctic. I am not sure that this White House would recognize a provocation if it was slapped in the face, and we need to be aware of that. Thank you, Mr. Chairman.

Senator REED [presiding]. Thank you, Senator Sullivan.

On behalf of the chairman, Senator Tillis.

Senator TILLIS. Thank you, Senator Reed.

Admiral Harris, thank you for the time that I was allowed to spend with you out in headquarters. We got a very thorough brief, so I am not going to cover that ground, but I appreciate it and I know that in your public statement, or your opening statement, and in the conversation you covered some of it.

I do want to get back and maybe build on questions that Senator Inhofe asked, and it had to do with the rebalancing where we are going out and saying that we are putting more assets as a percentage of the base into your area of command. We continue to miss the point that the base is shrinking. So part of what I am trying to do is get my head around a number of different variables that really let us measure the gap between China and the United States and our allies. You said when we were out there in the briefing that quantity has a quality of its own, so that right now we still continue to enjoy an advantage over the Chinese in terms of the assets we have in the region.

When you start trending out to 2020 and beyond and you take into account that they may have more ships but their survivability does not compare to our own and the technology onboard does not compare to our own, at what point does the gap, if you were projecting assuming sequestration was going to be in place—I hope that that is not true, but let us assume that we are and the current plans for downsizing. At what point do we really reach a point to where it is a fair fight or we may be at a disadvantage? I do not want us to be in a fair fight, incidentally. So I want to know when it is and then at what point does it erode to where we have a quantitative or qualitative disadvantage against China.

Admiral HARRIS. Yes, sir. I am all for having unfair fights, and I think that those fights out to be unfair in our advantage. I believe that if we are continued to be sequestered through 2021, 2022, and China continues the pace of its building, that their quantitative advantage will be significant in the mid-2020's.

Senator TILLIS. To overcome our qualitative advantage?

Admiral HARRIS. I think we will always have a qualitative advantage if we maintain the trajectory we are on. We have better trained people, better equipment, and all of that. As you said, quantity has a quality all its own. Their weapons systems and their ships and airplanes bristle with weapons, and they probably view them—view the loss of those ships in a much different way than we would view the loss of our ships and the sailors on them. So I am worried about the pace of the Chinese buildup against the likelihood or the possibility that we will continue to be sequestered, and I think that will pose a very real problem for us in the 2020's. I think that we should look at that very closely, sir.

Senator TILLIS. Has there been work done to try and put that on paper? It may not be appropriate for an open setting, but to take into account our own unilateral capabilities in the region, the added capacity of our allies. That is another advantage that we share there. We have allies. They do not really. Has there been anything at that level that I can put my hands on to really understand that and then the trending out into the mid-2020's? Secretary?

Secretary SHEAR. I think with regard to China, we put out the annual China military power report, and I think that is a good measure of where the Chinese have been and where they are going with regard to military modernization and their capabilities.

Senator TILLIS. Does that include a match-up against our projected capabilities assuming sequestration and the other policies that are the givens right now?

Secretary SHEAR. It does not, sir.

Senator TILLIS. That is more or less what I am talking about to try and figure out where the gap is and where we really have to sound the alarm that we are letting the margin of advantage erode.

Admiral HARRIS. Senator, the United States-China Commission, a body that is chartered by Congress, puts out an annual report that is exceptional in reading about China's capabilities. So I would commend that to you as well.

Senator TILLIS. Thank you.

Admiral HARRIS. As far as the allies go, we have five treaty allies in the Pacific of varying degrees of capability, but whether they would be with us in every fight is a matter for them to decide in the fight at hand. So while I count the delta in numbers between us and China, I try not to count the quantity of assets our allies have because, depending on the situation at hand and their own national decisions, we might have to fight alone.

Senator TILLIS. Thank you.

Senator Reed, if I may. I do not think it came up in the discussion, but either for the Ambassador or for Admiral Harris, to what extent do you believe that the trade agreement—in this particular case, the TPP [Trans-Pacific Partnership] and the partners there—is another key part of our military strategy down in the South China Sea and the Pacific?

Secretary SHEAR. It is definitely a key part of our strategy, Senator. The TPP is not just economically beneficial, but it is strategic, and I think our partners understand that. The Vietnamese certainly understand it. When I was Ambassador in Vietnam through last year, the Vietnamese had an acute understanding of the strategic importance of TPP. It will be one of the ways in which we further knit together Southeast Asian integration and ASEAN strength. Not all ASEAN members are TPP partners, but TPP will certainly raise economic activity through the region, and countries like Vietnam are among those TPP partners which will benefit the most.

Senator TILLIS. Thank you.

Senator REED. Thank you, Senator Tillis.

I have been informed that some of our colleagues are returning from a vote on the floor and would like to ask questions. That gives me the opportunity to ask a few questions until they return.

So, Admiral Harris, we have spent a great deal of time talking about the South China Sea, but India and Australia are actually conducting joint maritime exercises in the Indian Ocean, actually anti-submarine exercises, and presumably that is because of the presence more and more often of Chinese submarines in that area.

So can you describe these operations? Does this represent another challenge to the existing security arrangements in the area?

Admiral HARRIS. Senator, we are seeing Chinese submarine deployments extend further and further, almost with every deployment. It has become routine for Chinese submarines to travel to the Horn of Africa region, the north Arabian Sea in conjunction with their counter-piracy task force operations. We are seeing their ballistic missile submarines travel in the Pacific at further ranges. Of course, all of those is of concern.

With regard to India and Australia, Australia is one of our principal allies in the Indo-Asia-Pacific region, certainly an ally with tremendous capability. India presents a terrific opportunity for us, and one of the PACOM lines of effort is an improved mil-to-mil relationship with India. I am excited by the opportunities that we have with India by the work that the Secretary of Defense has done and Assistant Secretary of Defense Kendall has done with regard to the DTTI [Defense Technology and Trade Initiative], the defense initiative with India, to help them build up their military and help them build an aircraft carrier capability. So India presents a wonderful opportunity for us. They share out values and our norms, and one of my objectives is to improve that relationship with India.

Senator REED. This increased activity by Chinese submarines, both attack submarines and ballistic submarines—is that further stressing your submarine fleet in the Pacific, those ships that are available to you?

Admiral HARRIS. It is. It is clearly stressing it. The new Russian submarines that are moving into the Pacific fleet area—their Pacific fleet area also places a stress on limited assets that we have.

Senator REED. So we have to continue, obviously, to keep a robust submarine fleet, both attack submarines and ballistic submarines.

Admiral HARRIS. Absolutely.

Secretary SHEAR. Sir, I would like to——

Senator REED. Please.

Secretary SHEAR. If I may, I would like to add a little more on India.

When President Obama was in India for meetings with Prime Minister Modi in January, they issued a joint strategic vision on the Indian Ocean and East Asia. We are in the process of devising ways of implementing that joint strategic vision. I was in India through last Saturday for discussions with my counterparts on how to implement that vision. We already have a robust program, a robust bilateral cooperation with the Indians. The admiral mentioned DTTI. We also have a carrier cooperation working group that has begun to meet. I think cooperation in carrier technology and design, as well as in carrier operations, offers us a terrific opportunity to improve our ability to work with the Indians.

We will be looking at other ways of strengthening our partnership. We conduct an annual exercise, the Malabar Exercise, in which we and the Indians have just decided to include the Japanese. So that will be every year now. That will be a strong trilateral exercise in the region. We are looking at other ways, particularly in maritime domain awareness, to strengthen what we do with the Indians because we have very strong common interests.

Senator REED. Well, thank you, Mr. Secretary.

Just a further point—I have Senator Ayotte. If she is ready, I would be happy to yield.

Senator AYOTTE. That would be great. If you want to finish your questioning——

Senator REED. No. Thank you. At this point, let me, on behalf of chairman McCain, recognize Senator Ayotte.

Thank you, gentlemen.

Senator AYOTTE. I want to thank the ranking member. I appreciate it.

First of all, Admiral Harris, I want to thank you for following through and visiting the Portsmouth Naval Shipyard. I know that everyone at the shipyard was very appreciative of your taking the time to see the incredible work being done there on our attack submarine fleet. So thank you. We are grateful.

I wanted to ask in follow-up on some of the questions that you have been asked, Admiral. I think I understand from the testimony you have given, but I want to make sure that we are clear because I know that you have been asked about the Asia-Pacific maritime security strategy, that China's artificial islands could at most generate a 500- meter safety zone and that, of course, the Department of Defense had released a statement saying that these features under international law do not generate any maritime zones because you believe that they are not legitimate. What this means in practice is that the Navy actually can, as you know, sail its ships within 500 meters of these new land masses without violating the law because they are not legitimately there under international law.

So I wanted to understand. Is the Navy sailing within 500 meters of China's artificial islands at this point?

Admiral HARRIS. No, ma'am.

Senator AYOTTE. Has the Pacific Command at least sent Navy surface ships within 12 miles of China's artificial islands?

Admiral HARRIS. We have not.

Senator AYOTTE. So I guess the big question I think many of us are trying to get at at this point—and I do not know, Admiral Harris, whether you or Secretary Shear are the appropriate person to answer the question. Why not? Saying we are going to sail and fly where international law permits and then not doing it I am concerned leaves China with the impression that we are again going to say something but not follow through on our actions, and we are going to invite more aggression by the Chinese with the activities they have been taking that are in violation of international law and building these artificial islands. So I wanted to get your answer to that.

Secretary SHEAR. Let me elaborate a little on what the admiral said. In recent years, we have challenged every category of Chinese claim in the South China Sea, as recently as this year. We will continue to conduct freedom of navigation operations in the South China Sea.

Let me be clear on this point. Freedom of navigation operations are important for demonstrating our rights under international law, but freedom of navigation operation alone will not stop Chinese activities on these features. Preventing the Chinese from further militarizing those features is going to take a range of options, including freedom of navigation operations, and we are in the process of considering those options now.

Senator AYOTTE. Admiral, did you want to add to that?

Admiral HARRIS. I will just add that PACOM presents military options to the Secretary, and those options come with a full range of opportunities in the South China Sea. We are ready to execute those options when directed.

Senator AYOTTE. So you are waiting for, obviously, the administration to make the call on that.

Admiral HARRIS. Well, I mean, the freedom of navigation operation itself, as Secretary Shear said, is not a military-only device. It has a military component obviously because the military executes it. It has other elements to it which are derived by the Secretary and the White House. So we are waiting for direction, and I am comfortable and confident that the options that we presented are being considered equitably.

Senator AYOTTE. Well, as I look at the situation, though, I appreciate, obviously, Admiral, that PACOM—as the Commander, you would be waiting for direction from the White House. As I look at it, the Chinese have to be looking at this situation saying the United States has declared that under international law this is not legitimate and that we have the right to, obviously, put our vessels in these areas, but the Navy has not sailed within 12 nautical miles of the Chinese artificial islands at this point. So I think they get it both ways. So they are saying we are saying one thing, but we are certainly not willing to address where we have a free right to navigate. So I hope that we follow up with our actions on our words on this, otherwise I fear that the Chinese will continue their actions because otherwise they think, hey, why not?

My time is up, but I am going to submit for the record, Admiral Harris——

Senator REED. Senator, if you would like to take some more time.

Senator AYOTTE. Oh, thank you. I just had a follow-up on a totally different topic. Thank you. I appreciate it.

I wanted to ask both of you on a different topic, which is about our POW–MIAs [Prisoner of War–Missing-in-Action] and our recovery efforts. This is a very important issue. I know Senator McCain and Senator McCaskill have been focused on this as well, and I have been appreciative of working with them. Obviously, the Department of Defense has reorganized its recovery efforts and stood up the new Defense POW–MIA Accounting Agency, the DPAA, in January of 2015, just the beginning of this year. One of the explicit purposes of this new organization is to effectively increase the number of missing service personnel accounted for from past conflicts.

So I wanted to ask—of course, with your mission in PACOM, this is incredibly important because of our fallen heroes in the Asia-Pacific region including, according to DOD, over 83,000 Americans are missing in action, 73,000 from World War II, 7,500 from the Korean War. In New Hampshire, we had someone who was able to welcome home the remains of his uncle. This really moved me because we know how important it is to family members to have that kind of closure. Also 1,600 from Vietnam, including 42 from my State.

So, Admiral Harris, I know this came up in your advance policy questions. Can you give me an update on how DPAA is doing, what efforts we are taking? If both of you could let me know your commitment, as we look at this. China has a very important role here in helping us recover our fallen heroes. So could you help me on this?

Admiral HARRIS. Yes, ma'am. As you stated at the beginning, the Joint POW Accounting Command, JPAC, the chain of command was changed, and now it is DPAA. The chain of command—now it no longer reports to PACOM. It reports directly to an agency under DOD.

My responsibility as PACOM is to be in support of DPAA. The people in Hawaii who actually work at the facility there, the DPAA facility now, are the same people, and I think they are doing a great job. They just recovered a bunch of remains in one of the Pacific island battles, including the remains of a Medal of Honor recipient. PACOM's responsibility was to provide support for the airlift and all of that. I think that is a tremendous effort by them.

I acknowledge the importance of going after every POW- MIA case that is extant. I think China—we need to continue to work with China and with North Korea and the other countries over which our fallen are from all the wars.

Senator AYOTTE. One thing I wanted to also clarify, Secretary Shear—and I appreciate, Admiral Harris, your commitment to this—is I understand we do have an agreement that was formalized with the Chinese. At this point, we have been somewhat stymied of getting information that they may have about Korean War POW camp records. I understand that Mr. Linnington, who is the director of the DPAA, has or will be interacting with the Chinese Government. I wanted to know what efforts the administration will be making in supporting his efforts to facilitate that communication, as Admiral Harris says, to be able to bring those, our soldiers, home.

Secretary SHEAR. Ma'am, I strongly support the efforts of the DPAA to make the fullest possible accounting of our missing personnel. As Secretary to Vietnam, I participated. I visited recovery sites. I participated in recovery ceremonies. As Assistant Secretary, I support the efforts of the DPAA just as strongly. I am aware of Director Linnington's efforts in regard to China and more broadly. I support those efforts in discussions with my counterparts.

Senator AYOTTE. Thank you both for that commitment. I appreciate it. We do not want to ever forget and make sure that we can bring as much closure to our families and bring our soldiers home.

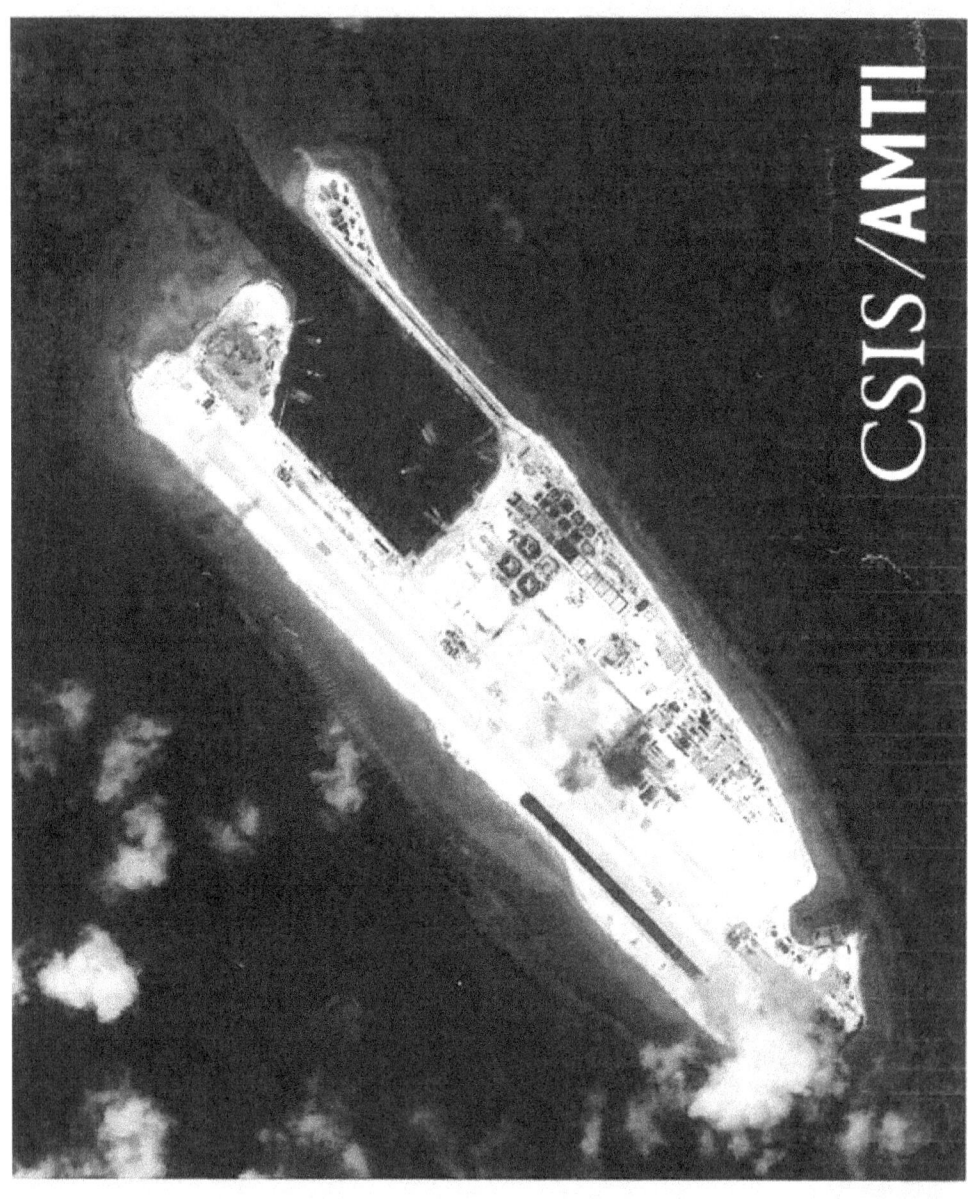

Senator REED. Thank you very much. Gentlemen, thank you for your testimony this morning, and on behalf of Chairman McCain, let me now adjourn the hearing. Thank you.

[Whereupon, at 11:41 a.m., the hearing was adjourned.]

[Questions for the record with answers supplied follow:]

QUESTIONS SUBMITTED BY SENATOR WICKER

QUALITY OF LIFE

1. Senator WICKER. In March 2012, I expressed concern to Admiral Willard that certain below standard dormitory buildings at Osan Air Base did not receive military construction funding in the fiscal year 2013 budget. I was specifically concerned about significant plumbing, lead concerns, and mold issues at Building 746, Building 708, and Building 475.

Will you provide the Senate Armed Services Committee and the Senate Appropriations Committee with an update on the overall status of enlisted dormitory housing at Osan Air Base as well as the specific status of Building 746, Building 708, and Building 475?

Admiral HARRIS. Building 475 has been demolished and Building 746 is unoccupied and scheduled for demolition. I am pleased to report that Building 708 has no record of lead or mold issues and its current HVAC and plumbing systems are fully mission capable. Additionally, all rooms in building 708 meet Air Force standards and are either occupied or ready for occupancy. The building is scheduled for a major overhaul in 2017 as part of a $4M dormitory refurbishment.

2. Senator WICKER. Also, what is the wing commander's assessment of the enlisted dormitory situation at Osan Air Base (active mission assigned personnel as well as support / tenant units)?

Admiral HARRIS. Overall, the 51st Fighter Wing commander assesses the condition of the unaccompanied housing at Osan Air Base as adequate to good. The commander additionally assesses there is no difference in the quality of dorms between those assigned to the 51st Fighter Wing and those assigned to tenant units. For context, Osan Air Base has 35 dormitories, including 33 for the Air Force and 2 assigned to the Army—a Senior NCO dormitory with 277 rooms and an Airman dormitory with 156 rooms. The base has an extensive facility repair and renovation program, with at least one dormitory under renovation per year, and a very robust dormitory furniture replacement program. Some of the dormitories were constructed in the late 1980s, and some individual rooms are closed for maintenance, however, none of the rooms are substandard. Individual rooms continue to have normal wear and tear issues, and residents are relocated as needed. At this time, all major systems are functional. The wing commander stated they are heading in the right direction and expects significant improvements to continue. I will personally visit one of the dormitories when I next travel to Osan Air Base.

3. Senator WICKER. Are there any plans to correct any substandard rooms remaining?

Admiral HARRIS. Today, 100 percent of dormitory rooms on Osan Air Base meet Air Force standards. At any given time, roughly 5 percent of rooms are empty for maintenance. However, these issues are addressed directly and residents are not moved into a dormitory room until it is ready for occupancy. The 33 dormitories on Osan Air Base, totaling 4,697 rooms, are managed through a robust 5-year plan incorporating both routine maintenance and major refurbishment. In total, there is $166M programmed for Osan Air Base dormitory projects over the next 10 years, with $79M of those projects programmed within the next 5 years.

———

QUESTIONS SUBMITTED BY SENATOR LEE

MODERNIZATION EFFORTS

4. Senator LEE. Admiral Harris, one of the themes of this week's Air Force Association conference that is taking place just down the road is the need to modernize our nation's air fleet to outpace the technological advances made by potential adversaries. In your opinion, looking at the current threat spectrum in the Pacific Command area of responsibility and the technological developments of militaries within

that area, how important is it that the service branches are given the funding and flexibility to modernize and address these threats? If you and future PACOM commanders are not receiving, training with, and maintaining the weapons systems that are designed to counter the types of military technology you will be facing in the future, what kind of risks will you be taking?

Admiral HARRIS. Funding, in many respects, defines our total military capability. I appreciate the support of Congress, and the opportunity to comment on this important issue. Continuous changes in fiscal assumptions due to budget uncertainty hamper our ability to plan. The result is poor use of resources. These uncertainties affect our people, as well as our equipment and infrastructure by reducing training and delaying needed investments. They directly affect our ability to pace threats by slowing investments in future capabilities. Services must have predictable and persistent funding to properly man, train, and equip a ready force. Additionally, Services must have the flexibility to develop and execute long-range programs for modernization while meeting current readiness needs. Funding uncertainties reduce warfighting capabilities, further reduce contingency response force readiness, and jeopardize our ability to meet the Defense Strategic Guidance. Uncertainty over funding ultimately risks the DOD's ability to fulfill USPACOM's commitment to the President's defense strategies. It jeopardizes our reach, and the lethality and technological edge we have today. It degrades our credibility as a reliable partner and imposes increased strain and risk to our service members.

REGIONAL COMMERCE

5. Senator LEE. Secretary Shear, you are well aware of the importance that Western Pacific maritime access is to U.S. commercial interests. More than $5 trillion worth of international trade traverses the South China Sea annually and the area is a significant site for the exploration and transportation of energy resources. What impact has Chinese action in the South and East China Seas had thus far on the free flow of commerce through that area, and what future actions could negatively impact this commerce?

Mr. SHEAR. Maritime Asia is a vital thruway for global commerce, and it will be a critical part of the expected regional economic growth. The importance of the Asia-Pacific sea lanes for global trade cannot be overstated. Eight of the world's 10 busiest container ports are in the Asia-Pacific region, and almost 30 percent of the world's maritime trade transits the South China Sea annually. Approximately two-thirds of the world's oil shipments transit through the Indian Ocean to the Pacific, and in 2014, more than 15 million barrels of oil passed through the Malacca Strait per day.

China is using a steady progression of small, incremental steps to increase its control over disputed areas East and South China Seas. This includes increasingly deploying the Chinese Coast Guard (CCG) to enforce its claims. For instance, China has used maritime law enforcement ships to restrict Philippine commercial fishing in the area of Scarborough Reef. The growing efforts of claimants, including China, to assert their claims has also led to an increase in air and maritime incidents in the recent years. Furthermore, China's land reclamation operations and infrastructure development over the last few years will enable it to establish a more robust power projection presence in the South China Sea. Broadly speaking, this has the potential to create uncertainty for not only the regional governments, but also for commercial entities operating in the region.

6. Senator LEE. Admiral Harris, does the Chinese military have the ability to close down some of these maritime routes in the event of a conflict, and what do you think could spark such an action from the Chinese navy? How would the United States respond to such an event?

Admiral HARRIS. [Deleted.]

CYBER SECURITY

7. Senator LEE. Admiral Harris, the Chinese and North Korean governments have both been involved in cyber-attacks and cyber-espionage against the United States Government and American businesses, and we are aware that cyber warfare will only become further engrained into future military doctrines. As a Combatant Commander, with these specific cyber threats in your area of responsibility, what do you view as your role in detecting, defending against, and deterring cyber attacks on the military personnel and assets under your command? What resources and authorities are you in need of to enable you to address this threat more effectively and proactively?

Admiral HARRIS. My role is to identify capability requirements that lead to military dominance in every domain, including cyber. To that end, I coordinate with United States Strategic Command (USSTRATCOM) and United States Cyber Command (USCC) in the employment of cyber warfare teams to deliver the needed capabilities in the context of a broader military effort. In ongoing operations, my role is ensuring that cyberspace operations are integrated, synchronized, and coordinated between USPACOM, Service components, the Defense Information Systems Agency (DISA), USSTRATCOM, USCC, and interagency partners who contribute authorities, capabilities, and insights critical to protecting infrastructure and information, detecting attacks, and deterring adversaries in cyberspace. I appreciate Congress' efforts to provide the resources that deliver technologies to provide strong, layered security and protection against the latest cyber threats. I am not aware of any unmet authority requirements that require Congressional attention at present. However, I urge Congress to continue to fund all cyber mission teams. While this may prove difficult under sequestration, it is vital to maintaining our ability to dominate in the cyber domain.

PACIFIC PIVOT

8. Senator LEE. Secretary Shear, one of the key elements of the military's strategy for shifting focus to the Pacific is having 60 percent of our naval and air fleets deployed to that region by 2020. Are we currently on schedule to meet this goal, and if the conflict against Islamic extremism continues at the same or an increased pace over the next 5 years, what impact will that have on the manpower and equipment levels available for operations in the Pacific?

Mr. SHEAR. The Department of Defense has worked to consistently implement President Obama's strategy of rebalancing toward the Asia-Pacific region. Over the past six years, we have made our engagement and investments in the Pacific a top priority, even in the face of budget constraints. The rebalance is first and foremost a whole-of-government approach, and we view our efforts as working hand-in-hand with the many political, economic, and development initiatives underway across the region.

To answer your question, the Air Force has already rebalanced to station 60 percent of its overseas air assets in the Asia-Pacific and Navy is on track to home-port 60 percent of the fleet in the region by 2020. Still, the hallmark of the rebalance is the emphasis on the quality, and not the quantity of our military presence in the Asia-Pacific region. We are actively investing in the future capabilities that we will need in the Asia-Pacific, including high-end capabilities. We are pushing our most advanced existing technology to the Pacific and we're finding new ways to use it. We're adapting our overall defense posture in the Asia-Pacific to be geographically distributed, operationally resilient, and politically sustainable. We are increasing the tempo of training and exercises in the region. We are modernizing the alliances and reinforcing the partnerships that are the bedrock of everything we do in the Asia-Pacific. All of this continues to occur amid a context of continued engagement in Afghanistan, as well as emergent efforts to counter Islamic extremism in the Middle East and strengthen defenses in Europe in response to renewed Russian aggression.

9. Senator LEE. Admiral Harris, the United States has longstanding alliances with many countries in eastern Asia from South Korean to India, and we participate in many military exercises, training events, military exchanges, and military assistance with these countries. What further benefit will the continuation of the pivot strategy offer the United States and our regional allies, considering the many engagements in which we are already involved?

Admiral HARRIS. One of America's key asymmetric advantages is that we have allies, partners and friends in the Indo-Asia-Pacific. Our principal adversaries do not. The Rebalance is key to this. The Rebalance is a strategic, whole of government effort that recognizes the vital interest that Pacific nations play in our future. The world is inextricably interconnected—the best way to maintain security, prosperity, and prepare for the future security environment is to maintain the positive momentum of the Rebalance and actively shape our national interests. The Rebalance is building trust and deepening our partnerships in the region, and it is always in our interest to have more friends. Surveys and opinion polls in the region indicate a strong desire for continued U.S. leadership and engagement in the region.

In recent years we have developed new or enhanced security relationships with most countries in the region, helped in no small part by our being a trustworthy alternative partner to offset China and North Korea's coercive and often unpredictable behavior. We have also helped improve the effectiveness of regional organizations and associated working groups under the ASEAN Defense Ministers Meeting Plus and ASEAN Regional Forum. These achievements, resulting from redoubled efforts under the Rebalance, are enhancing regional security and enabling regional militaries to contribute more in providing security in a region where complexity continues increasing.

As an example, our friends and allies across the Indo-Asia-Pacific are investing their own resources toward increased United States access. Of the four largest United States military construction efforts since the end of the Cold War—all in the Asia Pacific—Korea and Japan are contributing 82 percent of the cost: $30 Billion of $37B (Camp Humphreys, Korea; MCAS Iwakuni, Japan; Futenma Replacement Facility Okinawa Consolidation; Guam). Elsewhere Japan is providing 97 percent of Defense Policy Review Initiative (DPRI) construction funding in Japan ($16.9 B of $17.4B). U.S. investment in regional security is being reciprocated further by growing investments in U.S. military systems such as AEGIS ships, C–17, V–22, P–8, AH–64, UH–60, UH–72 and other aircraft, and other major hardware acquisitions that come with a decades-long partnership "tail" in training and logistics investments. The Rebalance is a sound investment that is paying dividends in terms of relationships, access, interoperability, stability and prosperity.

China continues its unprecedented military modernization, as demonstrated in South China Sea land reclamation and military acquisitions. North Korean nuclear development and provocations continue. Global terrorist networks are evolving faster than our allies and partners can counter them. Given the expanding threat, there is growing demand from allies, partners, and regional institutions such as the Association of South East Asian Nations (ASEAN) for engagement, partnering, training, and leadership from the United States. We must maintain our capacity to lead, further strengthen essential U.S. relationships, and shape the security environment. The Rebalance fulfills that need and is vital to our strategic future.

10. Senator LEE. Secretary Shear, how have the Chinese reacted so far to our pivot strategy in the Pacific and the Asia-Pacific Maritime Security Strategy? Do they perceive this as a threat, and as we continue towards PACOM's force structure goals, what further reaction can we expect from the Chinese?

Mr. SHEAR. For the past 15 years, China's military has pursued a comprehensive military modernization program focused on increasing its capabilities to conduct missions on its periphery and beyond to protect its perceived national interests and deter adversaries. We can expect this trend to continue for the foreseeable future, particularly because China's leadership views the strengthening and modernization of the People's Liberation Army as essential to China's broad objectives of achieving great power status.

The U.S. presence in the region has been a stabilizing factor since the end of World War II. Our presence is welcomed in the region by many because the military steps we are taking as part of the Rebalance to the Asia-Pacific region are intended to reinforce a rules-based regional order that is conducive to stability and prosperity for everyone in the region, including China. China's aspirations and the United States enduring presence in the Asia-Pacific region are not incompatible. We recognize that the United States-China relationship, as well as the military-to-military relationship, is characterized by elements of both competition and cooperation. Since 2012, China has responded positively to military-to-military engagement, resulting in improvements in the pace and scope of sustained and substantive exchanges that focus on risk reduction, as well engagements that expand our ability to cooperate in areas of mutual interest, such as counterpiracy, humanitarian assistance, and disaster relief. We will continue to focus our military-to-military engagements in ways that ensure that China acts in a manner consistent with international norms, resulting in outcomes that best serve the interests of the United States and our allies and partners in the region.

As the United States builds a stronger foundation for the military-to-military relationship with China, we will continue to monitor closely China's evolving military strategy, doctrine, and force development. Furthermore, we will continue to work with our allies and partners in the region to sustain the regional rules-based security order that has resulted in unprecedented peace and prosperity in the region for the past 70 years.

11. Senator LEE. Secretary Shear, how do you account for the possibility that such a large shift in military resources could inflame already tense regional problems? What will be our reaction if the Chinese military increases its military build-up in an attempt to offset our efforts?

Mr. SHEAR. The relationship between the United States and China is the most consequential in the world today. Pursuing a productive relationship with China is a critical element of the larger United States strategy for the Asia–Pacific region. The United States is a Pacific power that has vital interests in region, which we will protect through critical investments in our own capabilities, and the investments of our allies and partners.

United States leadership in the Asia-Pacific region is grounded in our treaty alliances with Japan, South Korea, Australia, Philippines, and Thailand. We have been modernizing these essential partnerships to tackle a full range of regional and global challenges. These alliances are powerful platforms for advancing a rules-based international system. The United States insists upon and will continue to underscore its fundamental national interest—one shared by our allies and partners—in preserving freedom of navigation and commerce through some of the world's busiest sea lanes. The United States will continue to sail, fly, and operate in accordance with international law in pursuit of our interests and those of our allies and partners.

We also have been working across the region to invest in regional institutions to strengthen the development of an open and effective regional architecture with the capacity to resolve conflict, support development and economic prosperity, advance human rights, and ensure that all countries in the region play by the same rules. United States support and participation in the Association of Southeast Asian Nations (ASEAN), the Asia-Pacific Economic Cooperation (APEC) and the East Asia Summit (EAS), and the Pacific Islands Forum (PAF) groupings are examples of our commitment to managing and reducing regional challenges.

The United States-China relationship is an integral component of our overall approach to the Asia-Pacific region. We recognize that there are elements of cooperation as well as competition in the relationship, which we will seek to manage through sustained and substantive dialogue and practical engagement in areas of mutual interest. The points of friction between China and the United States cannot be ignored, and we will continue to deal forthrightly with our differences.

12. Senator LEE. Secretary Shear, the United States officially does not take positions on sovereignty issues with respect to territorial and maritime disputes in the East and South China Sea. However, we are obligated by defense treaties to a number of countries that are currently involved in territorial disputes in this region. How would the United States respond to a hypothetical conflict over the Senkaku Islands, given our treaty obligations to Japan?

Mr. SHEAR. United States policy toward the Senkaku Islands, which was clearly stated by President Obama in April 2014, has not changed: Article 5 of our security treaty applies to the Senkaku Islands because they are under the administrative control of Japan. We consult regularly with our Japanese allies, and will oppose any attempts to change the status quo unilaterally.

————

QUESTIONS SUBMITTED BY SENATOR CRUZ

CHINESE MISSILE CAPABILITIES

13. Senator CRUZ. In his opening remarks, Chairman McCain said that the United States needs to "think anew about deterrence" in our relationship with China. This admonition is especially timely in light of China's recent military parade, an event which the People's Liberation Army used to unveil a number of new and updated ballistic missiles. Among them was the DF–26C, an Intermediate Range Ballistic Missile (IRBM) with a range of 3,000–4,000 km. Although concealed with a tarp during the rehearsal, reports indicate that the DF–26C appears to have three stages and a lengthy nose-cone. The latter feature suggests that the warhead may have a terminal guidance system, increasing its target accuracy. If true, this also introduces the possibility that China could introduce a fourth modification of the DF–26 similar to their "carrier killer" ballistic missile, the DF–21D. In 2012, The Diplomat highlighted the difficulty of AEGIS ballistic missile defense interceptors to engage a DF–21D in its midcourse flight due to possible decoys and in its descent phase due to its ability to maneuver at high speed. China reportedly tested the DF–21D successfully in 2014. The potential that the DF–26 now has a modification with terminal guidance introduces the troubling possibility that the United States is not only losing the anti-access/area denial competition in the South China Sea, but is actually ceding additional maneuvering space to the PLA.

Are you concerned about the ability of U.S. missile defenses to intercept the DF–21D and DF–26C throughout their course of flight?

Admiral HARRIS. [Deleted.]

14. Senator CRUZ. In Chapter 2, section 2 of the 2014 Annual Report to Congress, the United States-China Economic and Security Review Commission notes the observation of Hans Kristensen, director of the Nuclear Information Project and the Federation of American Scientists, that the Department of Defense (DOD) began reducing information regarding an estimate of the number of ballistic and cruise missiles in the 2010 "Military and Security Developments Involving the People's Republic of China" report to Congress. By 2013, this estimate had been completely removed from the annual report.

Why did the Pentagon begin removing its estimates of China's ballistic missile capacity in its 2010 report?

Mr. SHEAR. The Department of Defense's annual report to Congress on "Military and Security Developments Involving the People's Republic of China" continues to summarize the size, location, and capabilities of Chinese strategic land, sea, and air forces. This report is provided to Congress in both classified and unclassified form.

Details on China's missile systems in the Department's report have decreased as China has stopped publishing accurate figures on the numbers and types of its ballistic and cruise missiles. There are various unclassified estimates of China's missile inventory we could draw from, but those sources are not authoritative and may be inaccurate. The Department aims to provide the most accurate information possible to Congress; however, we must also weigh the potential risks to intelligence sources and methods should we reveal details regarding our knowledge of specific numbers of China's missile systems.

The 2015 annual report noted that China possesses at least 1,200 short-range ballistic missiles (SRBMs) in its inventory, and has an arsenal of 50–60 inter-continental ballistic missiles (ICBMs). The report summarizes the estimated range, key developments, and implications of China's ballistic missile systems.

The report also describes China's investment in anti-ship cruise missiles (ASCMs) and land-attack cruise missiles (LACMs). ASCM and LACM systems are further described by system type, operating units, and delivery platforms.

15. Senator CRUZ. Shouldn't Congress have an unvarnished estimate of China's military capabilities, particularly given their recent aggressive stance in the South China Sea and willingness to intrude into United States territorial waters off the coast of Alaska?

Mr. SHEAR. In addition to recurring testimony before defense oversight committees by senior Department of Defense officials, DOD provides an annual report to Congress on "Military and Security Developments Involving the People's Republic of China." This report is produced in partnership by the Office of the Secretary of Defense for Policy and the Defense Intelligence Agency. We coordinate the report with the Departments of State, Homeland Security, Energy, Commerce, and Treasury, and with the Intelligence Community and the National Security Council staff, so it reflects views that are held broadly across the United States Government.

We intend the report to be factual, descriptive, and analytical. We try not to speculate, but we let the facts speak for themselves. This report highlights China's military strengths and weaknesses, as well as the opportunities and the challenges that we see going forward.

Although the most recent Chinese movement of ships off the coast of Alaska occurred outside the period covered by the 2015 annual report to Congress, the 2015 DOD report did present a special topic section on "China's Reclamation in the South China Sea." That section described the size and potential uses of the reclaimed sites, and noted that "most analysts outside China believe that China is attempting to change facts on the ground by improving its defense infrastructure in the South China Sea."

RED FLAG AND RIMPAC EXERCISES

16. Senator CRUZ. On June 25, Chinese Defense Ministry spokesperson Yang Yujun expressed strong concerns at a monthly briefing about an amendment I introduced with Senators Inhofe and Wicker that called on DOD to invite Taiwan to Red Flag military exercises. In Yang's words, "We are firmly opposed to any country's military contact with Taiwan. Our position is consistent and clear." I believe that further military integration with Taiwan is imperative in reassuring our friends and allies and deterring the PLA from using force against Taiwan. Red Flag affords Taiwan an opportunity to participate in military exercises that will improve their self-defense capabilities and their ability to operate jointly with the United States, should that ever be required.

43

Do you plan to invite Taiwan to participate in the 2016 RIMPAC exercises? Do you plan to invite China?

Admiral HARRIS. (U//FOUO) We invited China to RIMPAC 2016, but reserve the right to cancel that invitation should our relationship deteriorate. We did not invite Taiwan to RIMPAC 2016, nor do we plan to. The nature of the relationship between United States Pacific Command and Taiwan's armed forces is not dependent on whether or not Taiwan is part of RIMPAC. Having said that, we will continue to maintain and deepen our strong military relations with Taiwan through continued exchanges and engagements in accordance with United States policy and the Taiwan Relations Act. I am a firm believer in, and supporter of, the Taiwan Relations Act.

17. Senator CRUZ. Does DOD intend to invite Taiwan to participate in Red Flag exercises?

Mr. SHEAR. The United States Government's approach to Taiwan has as its foundation the three joint United States-China Communiques and the Taiwan Relations Act. This approach has been a constant for eight U.S. administrations and will not change. Maintaining and deepening strong unofficial relations with Taiwan is an important part of United States engagement in Asia, a region of great and growing importance to the United States.

The Department of Defense engages closely with its Taiwan counterparts to support Taiwan's development of defensive capabilities to deter and, if necessary, resist coercion today and in the future. The United States has made available to Taiwan defense equipment and services in order to enable the island to maintain a sufficient self-defense capability.

This includes reviewing training opportunities for Taiwan to improve and maintain its readiness and operational capabilities. The Taiwan Air Force currently participates in several realistic and complex training scenarios each year at Luke Air Force Base with its F–16 aircraft that are designed to exercise defense counter-air tactics, formation flying, and attacks under simulated combat conditions. We do not believe it is necessary to invite Taiwan to Red Flag exercises at this point in time.

We believe this tailored training meets Taiwan's needs. We will continue to reassess Taiwan's capabilities and readiness levels to ensure that it receives the necessary training to maintain an effective defensive capability.

CHINESE LAND RECLAMATION

18. Senator CRUZ. Admiral Harris, when asked in Thursday's hearing for your opinion on whether the United States should sail or fly within 12 nautical miles of China's artificial islands in the South China Sea, you answered in part that the decision would ''depend on the feature'' of the land formation, referencing ''islands that are not islands.'' The Asia Maritime Transparency Initiative lists seven Chinese outposts within the Spratly Islands that exist on reclaimed reefs, specifically Cuarteron Reef, Fiery Cross Reef, Johnson South, Hughes Reef, Gaven Reef, Mischief Reef, and Subi Reef.

What is DOD's definition of what is and isn't an island?

Admiral HARRIS. The Department of State, through its Office of the Geographer, establishes U.S. policy on the legal status of geographic features. The DOS–Office of the Geographer has not yet released an official position on the South China Sea features. There are certain features, such as Mischief Reef, that we believe were originally below water at high tide, prior to China's massive reclamation. If that feature was originally underwater, then we can legally conduct normal operations, such as overflight and navigation in the vicinity of the features, including within 12 nautical miles. For other features that are legally characterized as either islands or rocks, we could not overfly within 12 nautical miles, but we could sail within 12 nautical miles in innocent passage.

The DOD definition of an ''island'' conforms to the definition stated in 1982 United Nations Convention on the Law of the Sea (UNCLOS). Although the U.S. is not a party to UNCLOS, it considers the navigation and overflight provisions reflective of customary international law and therefore acts in accordance with UNCLOS. According to Article 121 of UNCLOS, an island is ''a naturally formed area of land, surrounded by water, which is above water at high tide.'' An island is capable of sustaining human life and the status of a feature is determined by its natural formation and not by man-made alterations. An island is entitled to a territorial sea, an exclusive economic zone and a continental shelf. A rock is defined in Art 121 as a natural feature above water at high tide, which cannot sustain life on its own. A rock is entitled to a territorial sea, but not an exclusive economic zone or continental shelf. A low-tide elevation is a naturally formed area of land which is surrounded by and above water at low tide but submerged at high tide. A low-tide elevation is not entitled to a territorial sea, exclusive economic zone or continental shelf. Article 60 of UNCLOS clearly states that artificial islands, installations, and structures do not possess the status of islands and have no territorial sea of their own. Therefore DOD has the legal right to conduct normal operations within the vicinity of reclaimed features which were originally underwater.

19. Senator CRUZ. Do these seven reclamation sites fall under DOD's definition of an island?

Admiral HARRIS. The Department of State, Office of the Geographer is responsible for determining the official U.S. position with respect to the legal characterization all features, including reclamation sites. The U.S. currently takes no official position on the legal character of these seven reclamation sites, however we do not believe that all of them meet the legal definition of an island. We encourage the Department of State to take a position on the status of these reclamation sites and other features in the South China Sea. I would like to reiterate my point in question 18 that as a matter of international law, artificial islands and structures are not entitled to a territorial sea. We will conduct military operations in the vicinity of all features in accordance with international law.

QUESTIONS SUBMITTED BY SENATOR SHAHEEN

ELECTRONIC WARFARE

20. Senator SHAHEEN. Assured communications, particularly for command and control (C2) networks, is critical for our maritime forces. Our adversaries are becoming increasingly capable in electronic warfare technology, threatening our military effectiveness. Can you comment on the need to upgrade systems like the Link-16 with more advanced and adaptable anti-jam technologies while maintaining interoperability with legacy radios?

Admiral HARRIS. It is critically important; highly resilient, anti-jam encrypted communication technologies are necessary for command and control of forces operating within the air, land, and maritime domains and today's systems do not sufficiently repel efforts by adversaries to jam, exploit, or penetrate our legacy networks. Since Tactical Data Links (TDL) 16 and 22 are both based on technology developed decades ago, there is a pressing need to update or replace their technologies with new ones that will continue to be jam-resistant, provide cryptographic protection, and remain interoperable.

QUESTIONS SUBMITTED BY SENATOR HIRONO

PHILIPPINES

21. Senator HIRONO. The Philippines is one of the United States defense treaty allies in the Asia-Pacific and also a party to the South China Sea dispute with China. United States and Philippine armed forces regularly conduct joint land and sea exercises to boost security cooperation. How does the United States alliance in the Philippines fit in the overall maritime security strategy in the Asia-Pacific?

Admiral HARRIS. The United States-Philippines Alliance is a cornerstone of the Indo-Asia-Pacific security architecture, demonstrating the United States's commitment to peace and security for over 65 years, and it has a bright future in regional security. Through our historically close ties, we have developed a strong and cooperative relationship, which enables United States training and operational access to the South China, Sulu and Celebes Seas. I appreciate the Congress' creation of the Southeast Asia Maritime Security Initiative, which will significantly enhance our partnership by enabling greater investment in the regional security architecture, including improvements to the capabilities of the Armed Forces of the Philippines (AFP). The AFP's modernization will not only contribute to the security of the Philippines, but also provide substantive support and collaboration toward a regionally shared Maritime Domain Awareness. Furthermore, we continue to applaud and encourage the Philippines' use of international courts and arbitration to resolve maritime disputes.

Mr. SHEAR. A key element of DOD's approach to maritime security in Southeast Asia is to work alongside capable regional allies and partners. Through initiatives such as the Enhanced Defense Cooperation Agreement (EDCA) with the Philippines, the Department will be able to increase our routine and persistent rotational presence in Southeast Asia for expanded training with the Philippines and other regional partners. We are conducting more than 400 planned events with our treaty ally, the Philippines in 2015, and there is broad regional agreement on the importance of improving maritime security and maritime domain awareness capabilities in an effort towards promoting peace, stability, and prosperity in Asia. In conjunction with the Department of State and the United States Coast Guard, we have dramatically expanded our maritime security assistance and capacity building efforts in recent years. In the Philippines, the Department is providing coastal radar systems and assisting the Department of State with naval maintenance capacity building as well as providing interdiction vessels, naval fleet upgrades, communications equipment, and aircraft procurement. The Department is also working with our allies, Japan and Australia, in a coordinated fashion to maximize the efficiency and effectiveness of our maritime security capacity building efforts in Southeast Asia, beginning with the Philippines.

22. Senator HIRONO. Could you elaborate on how our recent sales of patrol vessels to the Philippine navy will enhance their capabilities and improve regional security?

Admiral HARRIS. The recent sale of Hamilton Class patrol vessels to the Philippines provides an initial credible maritime security capability, enabling the Philippine Navy to monitor and respond to maritime incidents and crises in their territorial waters and economic exclusion zone (EEZ). In tandem with their improving maritime domain awareness assets and sensors, Hamilton Class patrol vessels will extend their patrol range and improve situational awareness within their EEZ and adjacent waters enabling them to better protect their interests. In fact, I support the sale of a third Hamilton Class patrol vessel to the Philippines, should the opportunity arise. I had the opportunity to visit their new National Coast Watch Center (NCWC) in Manila (funded largely by DTRA) and was impressed by the potential that exists there. I believe that linking the Hamilton Class cutters to the NCWC will dramatically improve Maritime Domain Awareness.

Mr. SHEAR. The two United States Coast Guard High-Endurance Cutters (WHEC) that the Department of Defense transferred as excess defense articles to the Philippines in 2011 and 2013 supported a major non-NATO treaty ally and key alliance partner in the Asia Pacific region. The cutters' patrol capabilities have enhanced the Philippines' ability to contribute to humanitarian assistance and disaster response (HA/DR), respond to maritime domain awareness concerns, enhance interoperability with United States forces, and strengthen regional relationships by participating in multinational exercises. The United States and the Philippines also share the goal of ensuring freedom of navigation and unimpeded lawful commerce. By allowing the Philippines to patrol its Exclusive Economic Zone, the WHECs also support these shared principles and contribute to regional security. A combination of foreign military financing and Philippine national funds are being used to continue to enhance the capabilities of the WHECs.

23. Senator HIRONO. In July I introduced a bipartisan bill that would include the Philippines in the group of allied nations eligible for expedited consideration provided by law of foreign military sales. Currently that group includes just NATO, Japan, Australia, New Zealand, South Korea and Israel. Would you agree that the Philippines should be included in this group?

Admiral HARRIS. Yes. I strongly support adding the Philippines to the select group of allied nations eligible for expedited foreign military sales (FMS). The Philippines has been a staunch ally in enhancing regional security and supporting PACOM regional presence. Reducing United States Government processing time for government to government sales and commercially licensed arms sales would deepen our relationship and further improve our military ties, while accelerating progression in the capabilities of an important ally and partner.

Mr. SHEAR. Yes, the Department of Defense would fully support including our Philippine ally in the category of NATO countries for the purpose of congressional notification for foreign military sales. Although the Philippines is already designated a major non-NATO ally, inclusion in the NATO category would enable the Department, working with the State Department, to process Philippine foreign military sales cases more quickly by both increasing the threshold for congressional notification and shortening the timeframe of the required notification. Further, inclusion in this category would demonstrate the value and strategic importance of our Philippine ally.

GUAM ENERGY

24. Senator HIRONO. On July 14th, the Energy and Natural Resources Committee on which I serve held a hearing to examine the energy challenges that come from

living in places that are not connected to the rest of the country, including Hawaii, Alaska, and the U.S. Territories. We heard from Robert Underwood, the Former Guam Delegate to the House of Representatives. He explained that Guam relies on imported petroleum to serve most of its energy needs and that the local power companies are challenged to keep power constant. I visited Guam last month and heard similar concerns. What plans does the Navy have to enhance the resilience of the energy infrastructure needed to support the expanded military capabilities needed to develop Guam into a strategic hub in the region?

Admiral HARRIS. I appreciate the investments that Congress continues supporting on behalf of our national security interests in Guam, and I welcome every improvement that mutually benefits Guam and DOD. To that end, the Navy continues working with Guam Power Authority through master planning and partnerships that enhance the resilience of the Guam energy infrastructure. The Navy continues improving energy efficiency, reducing consumption, and partnering on renewable energy projects with Guam Power Authority, the responsible agency for Guam energy infrastructure.

Mr. SHEAR. The demand for electrical power under the military build-up can be met by the current generation capacity on Guam. No power generation upgrades will, therefore, be required. However, consistent with Navy sustainability goals, a portion of the power demand will be satisfied by power generated from renewable energy sources, including photovoltaic solar panels on rooftops and acreage within the cantonment and/or family housing areas.

We also plan to upgrade transmission lines and construct a new on-site substation.

Additionally, both the Navy and the Marine Corps recognize the need to reach and maintain security and resilience of the energy infrastructure. The Marine Corps is actively pursuing suitable ways of achieving that goal as well as providing a sensible approach to implementing renewable energy, with an objective of identifying practical and feasible energy measures that are reliable and financially reasonable.

FREELY ASSOCIATED STATES

25. Senator HIRONO. Last year I had the opportunity to speak with Secretary Carter, prior to his confirmation, about my concerns regarding our compacts of free association with the freely associated states (FAS) of the Federated States of Micronesia, the Republic of the Marshall Islands, and the Republic of Palau. We began our relationship with these nations after World War II, when we began testing nuclear weapons in the Marshall Islands. The U.S. was tasked with governing the region, then referred to as the Trust Territory of the Pacific, by the United Nations. It is worth noting that at one point the region was exclusively under the jurisdiction of the U.S. Navy. In 1986 these three nations gained their independence but remained strong allies of the United States through our compacts of free association.

The compacts ensured the United States would retain exclusive military jurisdiction over the region. It also allowed FAS citizens the opportunity to enlist in the military and freely travel between our nations. Recognizing that certain jurisdictions would be more likely to see an influx of FAS citizens, Congress provided dedicated funding to Hawaii, Guam, American Samoa, and the Commonwealth of the Northern Mariana Islands (CNMI) to defray the costs associated with this "compact impact."

In 2010, the United States concluded renegotiating the terms of our compact with Palau, in which we promised to provide $215 million to Palau through fiscal year 2024. While the compact is now in place, the United States has not ratified this agreement due to Congressional budgetary rules requiring a pay-for—in essence, the United States must find roughly $13 million annually to offset the costs of this promise.

According to the Department of Defense, FAS citizens generally, and Palauans specifically, enlist in the military at a higher rate than citizens of any State in the United States. I have met with Palauan President Tommy Remengesau, who has enumerated his concerns about China's growing economic influence and expansion in the Pacific and our seemingly lax attitude toward our compact with Palau. His concerns were clear: if the United States does not live up to its promises to Palau, how we will keep the region clear of China's influence?

I am sincerely concerned that our lack of action in this matter may pose a threat to our position in the region. This is especially worrying as China's influence in the region continues to grow –a concern which I believe provided the most compelling reason for the Department to rebalance its forces to the Asia-Pacific region. I would like to continue my conversation with Secretary Carter, as well as Admiral Harris, and Secretary Shear on this issue, and ask the Department to please consider the following questions:

Given the above, can you please elaborate on whether, and how, the FAS play a role in the Department's plans for its rebalance to the Asia-Pacific?

Admiral HARRIS. Assured and exclusive access to the Freely Associated States (FAS) plays an important supporting role in United States efforts to maintain much-needed influence from San Diego all the way to Southeast Asia which would be of vital importance in a contingency or conflict. The FAS are home to strategic facilities such as the Reagan Ballistic Missile Defense Test Site on Kwajalein, as well as key capabilities such as our Civic Action Team in Palau. FAS citizens are serving honorably in the U.S. military and beginning in 2010, are graduating from U.S. service academies. The FAS are strategically located and it is in our national interest to maintain strong ties with the FAS. The FAS will play an important role in the event of regional conflict as hubs to maintain open sea lines of communication. I support Congress' efforts to ensure our relationships remain steadfast.

Mr. SHEAR. Maintaining strong relationships with the Freely Associated States sends a strong signal about our commitment to the rebalance. As a whole, our three Compact agreements ensure that the United States has what essentially amounts to continuous air and sea access from the Philippines to Hawaii, which is important in supporting our ability to move forces in and out of the region freely.

26. Senator HIRONO. Does the Department share my concerns, which echo those of President Remengesau, about China's expansion into this region?

Admiral HARRIS. [Deleted.]

Mr. SHEAR. The Department of Defense is concerned with any activity, including Chinese activity, directed at disrupting United States relationships and access to the region. We welcome the appropriate involvement of other parties to address regional concerns, so long as their activities are conducted with transparency, accountability, and respect for international standards.

27. Senator HIRONO. Has the Department given any consideration to what losing the support of Palau or the other freely associated states would mean for the security of the Commonwealth of the Northern Mariana Islands (CNMI), Guam, or Hawaii?

Admiral HARRIS. Losing the support of Palau and/or the other two Freely Associated States (FAS) would create an opportunity for another nation to offer increased assistance to these countries and build additional influence which, over time, can only work to the U.S.'s strategic disadvantage. China is clearly pursuing a strategy to that end through offers of loans and economic development. The Compact agreements are individual and bilateral, and, because of geography, losing the support of any one of the three FAS would reduce our ability to protect the remaining two—something the U.S. promised to do in the Compacts. The defense relationship that USPACOM built with the Palauan Government through semiannual bilateral meetings has improved my confidence that Palau would support United States defense interests in a contingency situation. I welcome and support efforts by Congress to further deepen our relationship with the FAS, to ensure that our commitment remains unquestioned.

Mr. SHEAR. As a whole, our three Compact agreements provide the United States with what amounts to ensured air and sea access from Hawaii to the Philippines. Losing the support of Palau or the other Freely Associated States would lessen the broader strategic value of those arrangements in supporting our ability to pursue United States interests in the Asia Pacific region.

28. Senator HIRONO. Does the Department have any plans to work with other agencies, such as the State Department or the Department of the Interior, to come up with a comprehensive strategy to ratify our compact with Palau and secure our standing in the region?

Admiral HARRIS. DOD and USPACOM have a strong working relationship with Palau, and with both the Department of State and Department of Interior. I recognize Palau's strategic importance and will continue working to ensure that our relationship remains strong.

Mr. SHEAR. Congressional approval and implementation of the Agreement has been a priority for the Administration since the agreement was signed on September 3, 2010. The Department of Defense has worked with the Department of State and the Department of the Interior on developing a strategy to obtain approval of the agreement and will continue working toward that end state in support of State and Interior efforts.

29. Senator HIRONO. Are there areas in which the Department can assist jurisdictions impacted by migration from the FAS to States and territories, specifically Hawaii and Guam, in providing housing, economic development, or employment solutions for this population?

Admiral HARRIS. As you noted, we are fortunate that citizens of the Freely Associated States (FAS) take advantage of their opportunity to enlist in the United States military, serving honorably while supporting their families with military housing and other benefits. There is not a specific Department of Defense program directed towards the housing, economic development, or employment challenges facing the FAS population, but military commanders will continue their close coordination with local community leaders to explore mutually beneficial opportunities.

Mr. SHEAR. DOD does not have efforts underway directed specifically toward housing, economic development, or employment solutions for Freely Associated States (FAS) populations migrating to U.S. States and territories. However, many FAS citizens do take advantage of the opportunity to seek employment and housing benefits by joining the U.S. military.

30. Senator HIRONO. I've also recently met with businessmen from the CNMI, who discussed concerns with Chinese economic expansion in their territory—the same United States territory that is still without full power more than a month after a typhoon wiped out its power grid. I'm told that Chinese economic expansion in the region has been substantial. Would the Department consider economic expansion to CNMI a threat to security in the Pacific region?

Admiral HARRIS. Yes. PACOM is concerned by the growing influence China may be gaining through its economic engagement in the Pacific Island Nations. Current Chinese economic engagement could facilitate Chinese strategic interests in the region (particularly in the FAS), leaving the United States with reduced levels of access and influence. Chinese economic investment can drive growth, but it has also left countries, particularly small countries, with unmanageable debt.

Mr. SHEAR. The United States Government supports sustainable economic development for Palau. The Department of Defense is concerned about the possibility of any country, including China, using economic engagement to facilitate its strategic interests in a way that reduces United States access and influence. Although Chinese economic investment can potentially create growth, it may also burden countries, particularly small ones with unmanageable debt. Investment in CNMI by private Chinese enterprises obligations can be beneficial for economic development there, and in our view, would be compatible with our proposed military activities.

QUESTIONS SUBMITTED BY SENATOR KING

MILITARY CAPABILITIES IN THE ASIA-PACIFIC

31. Senator KING. What additional capabilities will the DDG–1000 class destroyer bring to our Pacific Fleet once in service, and how do you anticipate future commanders in the Pacific will employ these capabilities?

Admiral HARRIS. As extremely capable multi-mission combatants, the DDG–1000 class will provide future Pacific commanders a wide range of employment options to meet the challenging sets of warfighting and Theater Security Cooperation missions both on the open ocean and within the littorals.

The DDG–1000 class is under construction, and the first ship, DDG–1000, is expected to be operational in Fiscal Year 2019. Once operational, DDG–1000s will provide the next-generation multi-mission surface combatant capabilities tailored to provide land attack and littoral dominance to defeat current and projected threats. In the littoral region, the DDG–1000's two Advanced Gun Systems firing Long-Range Land Attack Projectiles will triple naval surface fires coverage to meet validated Marine Corps fire support requirements. Employing active and passive sensors and a SPY–3 X–Band Multi-Function Radar, DDG–1000 will conduct area air surveillance, including over-land coverage, in the traditionally difficult and cluttered sea-land interface region. Its Integrated Undersea Warfare suite coupled with reduced acoustic output will significantly enhance the ships' mine avoidance capability when operating in the littorals. DDG–1000 will also employ a composite superstructure which reduces radar cross section 50-fold. This, along with reduced acoustic output will make these ships harder to detect and improve survivability in an anti-access/area denial environment. I am excited about the operational capability these ships will bring to the Pacific.